A Handbook on Debt Management for Colleges and Universities

by

Robert T. Forrester
Coopers & Lybrand

NACUBO

One Dupont Circle
Washington, D.C. 20036

Printed in the United States of America

Edited by Yamile M. Kahn

Library of Congress Cataloging-in-Publication Data

Forrester, Robert T.
Handbook on debt management.

Bibliography: p.
1. Universities and colleges—United States—Finance—Handbooks, manuals, etc. 2. Universities and colleges—United States—Accounting—Handbooks, manuals, etc. 3. Corporate debt—United States—Handbooks, manuals, etc. I. Title.
LB2342.F65 1988 378′.02′0973 88-1679
ISBN 0-915164-38-8

Contents

Preface v

1 **History of College Debt** 1

2 **The Need for New Debt** 7

3 **Common Concerns with Debt** 11

Funded Depreciation and Debt Capacity 13

4 **Choosing a Source of Funds** 19

Debt Policies 20
Controlling the Financing Process 22
Blended Pool of Funds 25

5 **Credit Support** 29

6 **The Effect of the Tax Reform Act** 31

Tax Reform and Its Impact on Supply and Demand 31
The Effect of Tax Reform on the Structure and Marketing of Tax-Exempt Bonds 33
The Choice between Variable-Rate and Fixed-Rate Bonds 34
Asset/Liability Management: Caps, Swaps, and Self-Insuring Interest Rate Risk 35
Timing, Call Options, and Refunding Strategies 38
Taxable Financing Alternatives 40

7 **Accounting Issues over the Life Cycle of Debt** 43

Premiums, Discounts, and Costs of Issuance 43
Debt Service Reserves 44
Allocation of Debt Service among Projects 45
Treatment of Construction in Process 45
Other 45

Life Cycle Considerations 46
Capitalization of Interest 47
Extinguishment of Debt 50

8 **Federal Recovery** **57**

APPENDIXES

1 **Examples of Debt Accounting** **63**
A. Bank Financing 63
B. Tax-Exempt Financing 69

2 **Questions/Interpretations Regarding Debt Accounting** **79**

3 **Subject Bibliography** **85**

Advantages/Uses of Debt Financing 85
Debt Capacity 86
Capitalization of Interest 87
Defeasances 87
Debt's Relation to Overall Financial Management 88
When Debt Financing Goes Bad 89
Accounting Issues Related to Debt 89
Miscellaneous 90

4 **Criteria by Various Credit-Rating Agencies** **91**

5 **Hospital and University Credit Ratings** **95**

6 **Features of Tax-Exempt Financing Alternatives** **97**

7 **Significant Features of the Tax Reform Act of 1986** **103**

Five Percent Private Activity Limit and Costs of Issuance 104
Arbitrage Requirements and Reserve Restrictions 105
Refundings 106
Miscellaneous Tax-Exempt Items 106

8 **Example: Choosing a Source of Funds** **107**

9 **Example: Capitalization of Interest** **109**

10 **Example: Gain on "Low to High" Refunding** **111**

Notes **113**

Preface

Debt is growing rapidly on the balance sheets of American colleges and universities. Between 1983 and 1986, colleges and universities issued about $20 billion of debt.[1] With this level of debt, any new recession could bring about defaults. It is no wonder that university treasurers are more concerned about debt capacity than ever before and that college and university accountants are finding that previously insignificant nuances of debt bookkeeping have become matters of more than routine concern.

Even so, colleges and universities are not likely to stop issuing debt soon. There is a wide consensus that billions of dollars of new debt will be needed to renew facilities. A leading commentator has suggested that $36 billion is needed to renovate unsatisfactory space—with another $3 billion per year needed just to maintain the 80 percent that is currently adequate.[2] Recently, debt has also played a growing role in supporting students. Supplementary student loan and tuition-financing programs will shift some of the burden from individuals to the institutions their children attend.

At one time, colleges sought financial equilibrium in one relatively simple form: a balanced operating budget. Today, university business officers are striving to make sure that the capital structure at their institutions is also in balance. Some believe that the demands of the debt service related to added facilities and student-financing debt could lead to an imbalance in institutions' financial equilibrium in the future.

It is not surprising, then, that some of the questions received most frequently by the Accounting Principles Committee of the National Association of College and University Business Officers (NACUBO) refer to managing and accounting for debt. Treasury managers ask about the effect of debt on their institution's financial structures; controllers ask about the intricacies of accounting for it.

It is impossible to put into one volume all the material available on college and university debt.[3] This book is an attempt by NACUBO to create a handy reference manual for both treasury and controllership personnel. The first five chapters should be useful for the treasury officer who can use a primer in discussing college debt with top management or the board.

Chapter 1 is a short history of university borrowing. The exhibits in this section show how recent borrowing trends in higher education have paralleled those in the U.S. commercial sector.

University debt may be at its highest level, but the need for new debt for building renovation and student financing may well exceed obligations now outstanding. Chapter 2 discusses this need for new debt, principally for facilities.

The principal concerns with growing debt levels are (1) How long can debt keep growing? and (2) Will it ever be repaid? For treasurers whose boards are asking these questions, chapter 3 offers some answers. For example, debt can grow as long as institutional borrowers remain creditworthy; to accomplish this, management and trustees must develop borrowing policies that protect the institution's credit rating. Chapter 3 compares the potential effect on the university's debt capacity of charging depreciation, instead of debt service, as an operating expense.

Chapter 4 discusses blended pools of debt. Rather than associating debt with specific projects, universities of the future, like corporations, will seek the most efficient overall capital structure, composed of a blend of debt and equity from operations, gifts, and other sources.

Bond insurance, discussed in chapter 5, may ensure access to the capital markets and should become available more widely with the formation of the College Construction Loan Insurance Association (CLIA). The federal government, through taxation as well as indirect cost-recovery policies, will continue to have a major effect on universities' debt structure. Chapter 6 discusses debt after tax reform.

The last two chapters will probably interest the controller's office more than the treasurer's. Accounting for the debt life cycle, including capitalization of interest and defeasance, is relatively straightforward and can follow the model described in chapter 7. Chapter 8 deals with federal recovery. Those who desire a handy reference to measures of debt capacity, types of taxable or tax-exempt financing, or accounting entries for debt will find them in the appendixes.

Chapter 1
History of College Debt

Although American municipalities have been borrowing since the early 1800s, tax-exempt debt did not take on its present character until the passage of the Revenue Act of 1913. This act excluded interest income on municipal issues from taxation. In the 1920s, state colleges and universities incurred some debt. Because it was unclear to what extent universities could commit their affiliated governments to an obligation to repay debt, however, borrowing was limited.

In the 1930s, the federal government's subsidization of public buildings led to an expansion of state institutions, while private colleges found it difficult to expand without donor support. Throughout this period, a trend persisted wherein private and state universities financed self-funding projects such as dormitories and garages with revenue bonds, and community colleges borrowed by means of publicly approved bond issues to be repaid through local taxes. (Generous gifts during this period financed the residence halls at some private universities. In the 1980s, Harvard renovated its residential houses with debt, at a cost three or four times that of the original construction.)

By the 1940s, revenue bonds, which establish limited obligations to repay, had become the principal debt-financing tool of colleges and universities. Still, borrowing was not the generally practiced method of financing capital plant until the start of the federal lending programs in the 1950s. By the early 1970s, federal programs had dwindled; they were replaced by bonding and building authorities, which issued tax-exempt debt for the benefit of both public and private higher education.

The beginning of the 1970s saw another change in college borrowing. In 1969, Congress enacted Section 103 (c) of the Internal Revenue Code (the Arbitrage Laws), which limited the investment of unused bond proceeds. By 1979, the federal regulations regarding issuance of tax-exempt securities under this section had been finalized. The 1975 default scare in New York City made the public aware that debt securities, including those of colleges and universities, were not risk free. Finally, the Tax Reform Act of 1986 placed significant limitations on earnings from the investment of unused bond proceeds and capped the borrowing capacity of major universities.[1]

EXHIBIT 1
History of College Debt

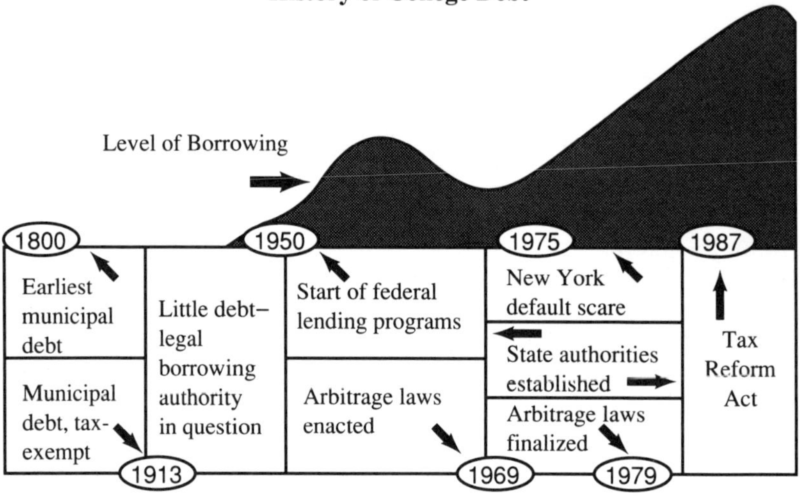

Source: Patricia A. Leary, Eastern Michigan

Exhibit 1 broadly summarizes these events. In analyzing the trends, one finds that the level of university borrowing has not been unlike that of consumer and other debt in the economy as a whole. From 1965 to 1981, debt and the gross national product (GNP) rose at approximately the same rate, and their ratio remained about flat between 1.3 and 1.4. Since 1980, however, the ratio of debt to GNP has climbed steadily to about 1.7 times the GNP (see exhibit 2).

While most universities have borrowed nowhere near their GNP level—that is, a year's operating budget—the trend in their debt levels is closer to that of corporations.

Exhibit 3 compares corporate borrowing as a percent of net worth to the debt of 15 endowed universities as a percent of plant equity. Adjusting this chart for an average six-month gap in the fiscal year ends of corporations and colleges, one can see that the trends are indeed very close.

Borrowing in 1985 (when there was deep concern about the continued ability to borrow under the tax laws) reached a high of $11 billion, or about 5 percent of the tax-exempt volume. While borrowing declined to less than $6 billion in 1986, the 1984-86 total is many times the previous three-year high and exceeds the growth in endowments during the period (see exhibit 4).

EXHIBIT 2
Ratio of Debt to GNP

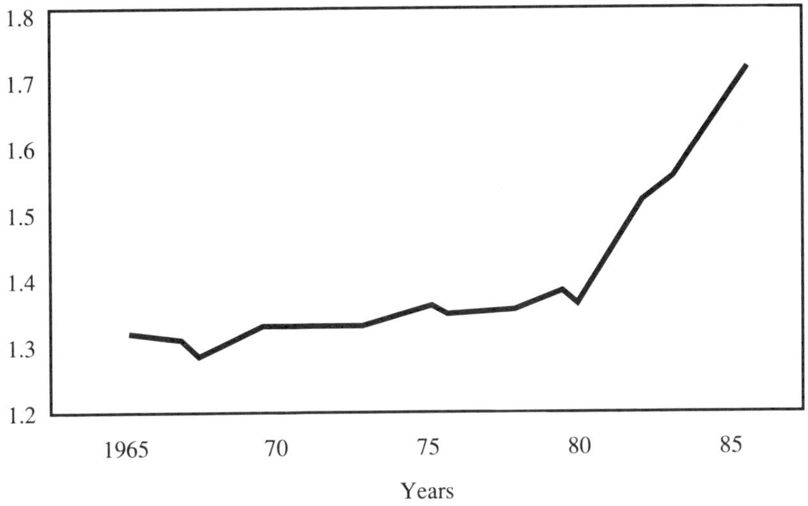

Source: U.S. Federal Reserve Board.

EXHIBIT 3
Growing Debt Levels

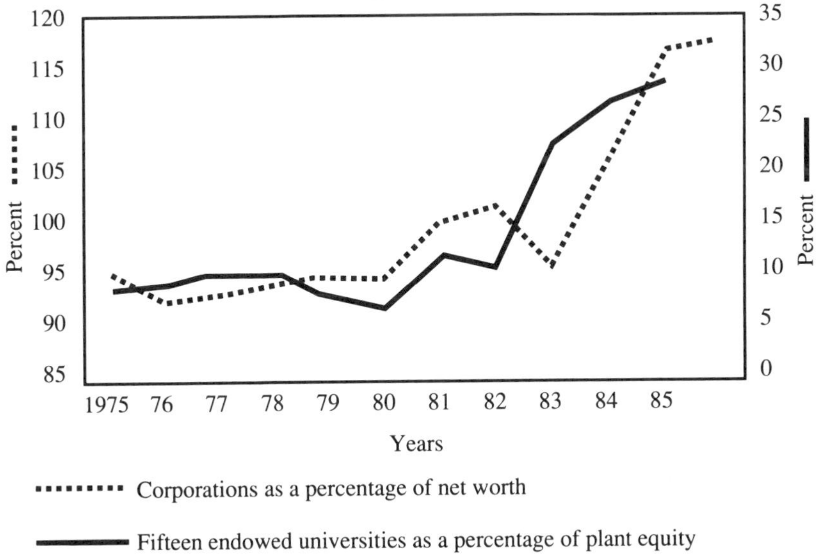

Sources: U.S. Federal Reserve Board; Cambridge Associates.

EXHIBIT 4
Historical Comparison of Tax-Exempt Financing and Higher Education Financing 1970–September 1986

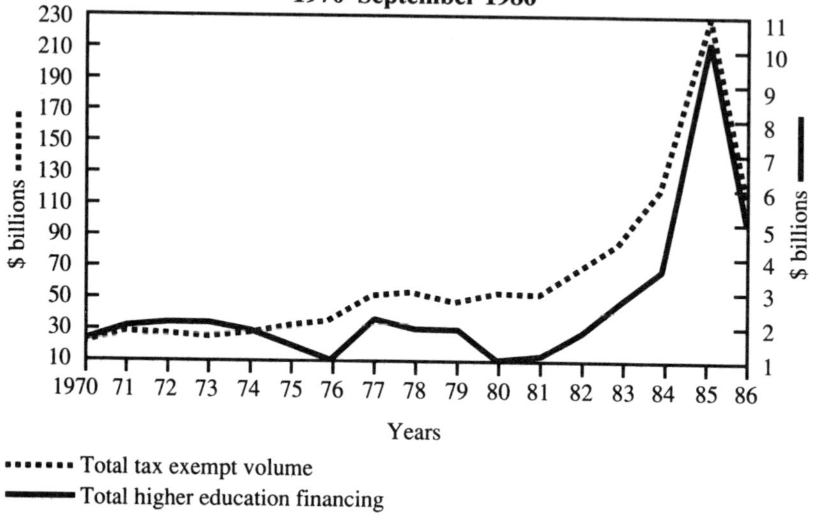

Source: Information Services, Inc.

During the 1980s, innovative financing mechanisms were designed to lower the cost of capital.[2] One type of financing involved securitization, a catchword for many of today's financings, which took the form of collateralized bond issues. The practice of collateralizing debt issues with unrestricted endowment fund assets was not new, but it enabled colleges to secure higher bond ratings and lower borrowing costs. Another type of financing involved variable-rate bonds. These made it possible for borrowers to capture interest rate savings by pricing debt on the low-cost, short-term end of the tax-exempt yield curve. Variable-rate bond issues also permitted issuers to earn the maximum levels of then-permitted arbitrage. The appeal of these issues was considerable: In 1985, colleges and universities issued about $4 billion in variable-rate debt, which represented a large portion of all higher education bonds sold (see exhibit 22).

Other innovations were designed to create financial instruments that had special features attractive to important investor segments, including zero-coupon and deferred-interest bonds.

Colleges and universities, along with other borrowers in the tax-exempt market, became experts at combining several varieties of these creative financing techniques into a cohesive package that minimized the overall cost of borrowing. Among the innovative packages developed, pooled financings offered small colleges access to a broader investor market at lower costs than these institutions could otherwise command. Under the pooled loan structure, a borrowing entity—often a state authority—would issue bonds in its own name and re-lend the proceeds to participating colleges. A third-party credit enhancement, bond insurance or a letter of credit, would typically overlay the pledge of revenues from the participants. Thus the bondholder could look to the credit provider rather than to each individual pool participant for security, and the pool would be rated based on the credit provider. This mechanism greatly increased the number of investors interested in purchasing the bond issue. Many pooled loan issues were initially structured as variable-rate bonds to achieve the maximum arbitrage spread in the loan-up period; these investment earnings were then used to offset many of the costs associated with the structuring of the loan pools.

College and university debt has grown significantly in the last few decades. As it has grown in volume, it has also become more sophisticated. Access to debt places new demands on, and creates new opportunities for, the chief financial officers of colleges and universities.

A major goal of the 1986 Tax Reform Act was to reduce abuses of the then-current tax system. Another was a need to increase tax revenues to offset the new lower personal tax rates. And, in fact, it was the collective judgment of Congress that there were abuses in the tax-exempt market. Specifically, the ability to earn arbitrage profits and the use of tax-exempt debt to finance private activities, while legal, were considered potentially abusive, and significant restrictions were imposed. Specific restraints on *higher education* tax-exempt financing were modest and applied generally to the larger, independent institutions. Higher education issuers should be aware of the continuing congressional scrutiny in the tax-exempt markets.

Chapter 2
The Need for New Debt

Institutions may borrow for a variety of reasons. Most commonly, debt is used to finance the acquisition of a physical facility. It can also be a source of working capital or used to help parents pay college bills. A few institutions may even borrow to pursue a profit-making venture.

Even though borrowing has grown significantly in recent years, the need for capital improvements in higher education continues. For some time, Harvey Kaiser of Syracuse University has catalogued studies of higher education plant and equipment around the country. These studies consistently show that about 20 percent of the facilities are unsatisfactory, and that estimated renovation costs reach into the billions (see exhibit 5).

In terms of constant dollars, building additions have decreased by over 50 percent. Current-dollar expenditures are relatively flat. After a ten-year flat period, however, equipment additions have increased by some 50 percent (see exhibit 6).

EXHIBIT 5
Need for Renovation

		Percent of Square Feet Unsatisfactory	Estimated Replacement Cost ($ millions)
1974	National	20	NA
1982	North Carolina	17	$301.6
1983	California	NA	$2,000
1982	Texas	NA	$301
1983	Indiana	24	$3,340
1985	Maryland	NA	$224
1982	New York	20	NA
Various	Kansas/Iowa/Arkansas	10–15	NA
1984	Columbia University	NA	$247

Source: Harvey Kaiser, Syracuse University.

EXHIBIT 6
Additions to Plant Value at Colleges and Universities 1971–84

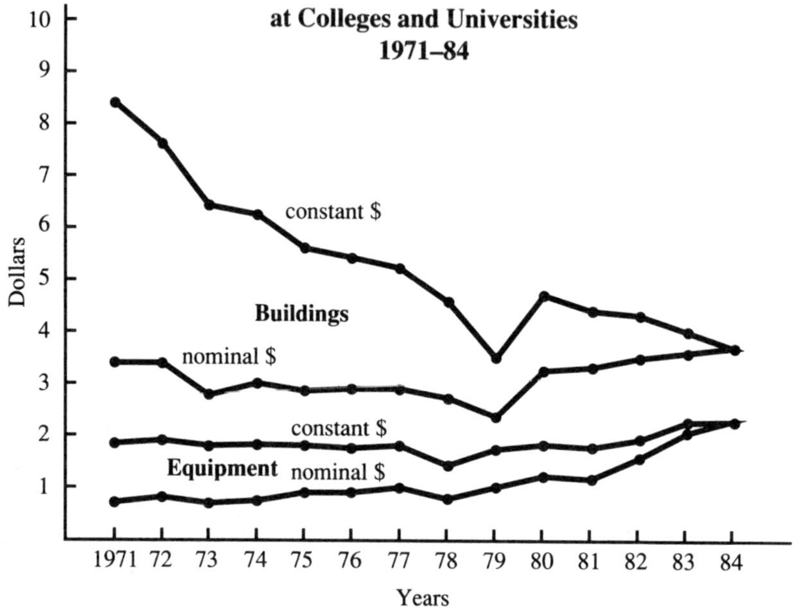

Source: National Center for Education Statistics, quoted by Harvey Kaiser, 1986.

In the nonprofit sector, universities are not alone in their need for debt. It is interesting, for example, to compare the sources of funding for colleges in a relatively prosperous period (1985-86) with that of hospitals in a similarly prosperous period (1981). According to Kaiser, about 30 percent of new construction work in process at colleges and universities in 1985-86 was funded by debt, while debt financed almost 70 percent of construction at hospitals (see exhibit 7).

Elementary and secondary schools also require new infusions of capital. Recently, Robert F. Wagner, Jr., president of the New York City Board of Education, estimated that "bringing the City's school buildings into the 20th Century" would require $4.2 billion in the next ten years, while a special commitment to spend $16.1 million in surplus funds from a municipal assistance corporation in 1986 would "hardly make a dent." With this commitment, the schedule for painting schools would remain the same—once every 33 years.[1]

Although other sources of funding besides debt exist, sufficient and broad access to these sources is uncertain. Federal and state governments, of course, continued their support of *new* construction in the

EXHIBIT 7
Sources of Funding for New Construction

	College Projects in Progress 1985–86 (percent)	Hospitals 1981 (percent)
Federal	10	12
State	40	
Debt	30	69
Private	7	4
Operations and other	14	15
	100	100

Source: National Science Foundation quoted by Harvey Kaiser; Ron Mulner, Dale Matthews, Joseph D. Kubal, and Steven Andres, "Debt Financing: An Alternative for Hospital Construction Financing," *Healthcare Financial Management* (April 1983), p. 20.

1970s, but government funding of plant renewal was inadequate. And as facilities grew, relative support tended to decline. Kaiser points out that capital outlays by state and local governments as a percent of gross additions to university plant decreased from 64 percent in 1970 to 51 percent in 1984. There is little evidence, moreover, to suggest that the federal and state governments will fill the current capital needs of higher education with direct appropriations.

Higher education, particularly the public sector, will continue to rely on public support. This support may take the form of a capital appropriation or the funding of debt service. The balance between these two types of support needs to be considered carefully by financial officers of public institutions.

Moreover, there are other reasons for a college or university to incur debt besides the financing of facilities. Many colleges need to borrow working capital—typically during the summer months before fall tuition revenues materialize. This is a routine if not totally desirable practice: An occasional cash shortage is hardly an indication of financial stress. If an institution has already severely stretched its debt capacity, however, an unexpected cash need could become a crisis.

Some institutions may want to borrow to finance an entrepreneurial activity if an opportunity arises. Although this leveraging increases the risks, it also increases the potential return.

In addition, one can expect an increased demand to finance students and their parents over the coming years. Recently, a number of institutions have increased their participation in parent-loan programs. In many of these cases, the institution does not borrow itself, but sells the loans to a state authority. Since the colleges are contingently liable for defaults on the loans, these loans may consume a portion of a university's debt capacity. Another current idea is "tuition futures." In some plans, the college may be responsible for any shortfall between the price of tuition and accumulated investment earnings in any particular student's fund. Colleges may be forced to borrow to meet the shortfall. Finally, a number of institutions are providing loan forgiveness for social service employment.

Since financial officers are likely to find a number of uses for debt, they must carefully examine the capital structure of their institutions and project the amount of each type of need into the future.

Chapter 3
Common Concerns with Debt

Because debt has grown so rapidly in the recent past, it is not unreasonable to find misgivings about its growth among management, trustees, and other concerned observers of higher education. Some question the prudence of debt. To them, debt is a sign that colleges, universities, and state systems have not disciplined themselves and adequately prepared for foreseeable capital needs. Some question whether debt levels can keep growing and if the debt will ever be repaid.

Unfortunately, there is too much truth to the idea that higher education did not adequately prepare itself for its current and future capital needs. But this observation is an exercise in hindsight. The 1970s were marked by a relatively weak economy and escalating inflation. There was also intense pressure to fund innovative programs for new students. These factors placed tremendous strains on the operating budgets of universities and made farsighted capital budgeting very difficult.

The mistakes of the past cannot be wished away; they only underscore the need for thoughtful and comprehensive capital budgeting in the late 1980s and 1990s. Moreover, not all of the capital needs were foreseeable. The emphasis on technology exploded in the 1980s, and now higher education is being asked to assume an expanded role in regenerating the economy.

Given these opportunities and challenges, higher education officials must ask two basic questions before incurring debt. Do the opportunities made available by debt financing exceed the costs? And, What is the nature of the risks if planning assumptions are wrong?

The cost-benefit questions can be asked in two ways. Specifically, each individual capital need may be available if an institution has the appropriate facilities. A relatively straightforward technical analysis can determine whether the funding can pay the necessary debt service. Administrators can then determine whether the prospective funding is secure enough to proceed. There are, however, risks and probably lost opportunities if an institution acts simply on a case-by-case basis.

A more generic approach, and one that is fast gaining popularity among large institutions, is to ask how debt fits into the overall capital structure. If, for example, an institution, the state, or both, are expanding, it is unlikely that past revenues could support all the capital needs of the institution. Growing enrollments or growing research programs suggest that the potential return on opportunities exceeds the current cost of capital. In a more stable situation, one would expect the institution to finance more renewals from internal sources. While the risks of a revenue shortfall on any one project may not be very great, the chief financing officer must consider the risks collectively from the institutional financial structure. Debt is just one of the sources of capital that the institution can use. The recent tax reform legislation adds to this need for integrated financial planning as it limits arbitrage possibilities and access to the tax-exempt markets.[1]

If there are sound reasons for using debt, can the debt be expected to grow without bounds? Upon reflection, one reaches the conclusion that debt can keep growing as long as borrowers are creditworthy and individual borrowings will be repaid, even though aggregate debt may grow. Perhaps the best way to illustrate the economics of debt is with a simple example from an article on the federal deficit that appeared in the *New Yorker*.[2]

Assume that the local telephone company (NYNEX) buys 1,000 telephone poles at $1,000 apiece. It finances the purchase with $1 million of debt, to be repaid at the end of ten years, with annual interest payments of $100,000, or 10 percent.

In years one through nine, the phone company must earn, at a minimum, enough revenue to cover the interest of $100,000 and to put aside depreciation of $100,000. In year ten, the phone company uses the accumulated depreciation to buy new telephone poles and borrows another $1 million to pay off the first investor.

The provision for depreciation was necessary in order to replace the financial capital invested in telephone poles. But because of inflation, it was probably not sufficient to keep up with the need to maintain physical capital. A million dollars is not likely to buy a thousand telephone poles in year ten.[3]

In addition, NYNEX would earn interest on the depreciation fund during the ten-year period. Hence, in the real world, in ten years the new telephone poles might cost $1.9 million, while only $1.45 million would be available, from depreciation and the earnings on depreciation, to finance them. This means that, in year 11, the telephone company would have to borrow $1.45 million to finance its new telephone poles.

If NYNEX were able to borrow this increased amount, it would be able to replace its poles. New debt would replace old debt; an individual debt issue would be paid; but aggregate debt would grow.

EXHIBIT 8
Comparison of Operating Statements of Two Enterprises

	Enterprise Charging Depreciation (NYNEX)	Enterprise Charging Debt Service	
		Year I	Year II
Revenue	$200	$150	$285
Interest expense	(100)	(100)	(190)
Depreciation	(100)		
Principal		(50)	(95)
Interest income	$ 45		
	$ 45	0	0
Replacement cost / New programs / Reserves	(45)		
	0		

Funded Depreciation and Debt Capacity

The telephone company (as well as a college or university) would be able to complete the cycle and replace its productive capacity if it were able to pay interest during the ten years and retain its debt capacity. Retaining debt capacity is generally regarded as a function of (1) maintaining liquidity and (2) managing leverage. Creditors and rating agencies measure liquidity and leverage in order to determine whether a new debt will be paid.

With regard to liquidity, creditors would look to see that the cash flow from depreciation was retained. Leverage must be managed because the aggregate debt will increase from inflation. In this example, NYNEX charges at least enough ($200,000 per year) for telephone service to pay interest and absorb a depreciation charge (see exhibit 8). Put another way, it funds its depreciation so that it is available to help buy new assets in the future.

By tradition, American colleges and universities have neither recorded nor funded depreciation. Of the many reasons, two are relevant to the discussion of debt. First, many institutions have demonstrated their ability to raise capital funds through contributions. Second, academic plant does not seem to be consumed like telephone poles. Buildings last many decades, even hundreds of years.

Instead of depreciating their plant, most universities have employed a funds-flow concept of financial reporting. Under this model, they record a charge for debt service (principal and interest) rather than depreciation. Exhibit 8 compares the operating statements of an enterprise that charges (and collects cash for) depreciation and one that charges debt service instead.

In the first year, assuming a level of debt service, revenue of $150,000 will be necessary to break even after charges for interest expense and principal repayment. This is less, of course, than the $200,000 required with depreciation. In the 11th year, however, new assets must be purchased at an inflated price. Then, revenue of $285,000 will be necessary to cover interest expense and principal on a sum borrowed (which, in the telephone pole example above, would be assumed to be $1.9 million because no depreciation fund was available). It will take more equity to support $1.45 million than $1 million of borrowing. This means that net assets must increase in excess of depreciation, either from operations, contributions, or interest income on reserve funds. In the case of the phone company, contributions of capital may come from shareholders; at the university, from gifts.

Revenue equals or exceeds interest expense plus depreciation. A commercial enterprise that is breaking even either retains depreciation in cash or spends it for new plant. If the depreciation is retained in cash, the organization will generate interest income. If it is spent for plant, that plant will generate more cash. Hence, funding the provision for depreciation assists the phone company in managing its leverage.

In a measurement of financial capital in the current structure of generally accepted accounting principles, depreciation will be taken on historical cost. A question often asked is whether depreciation should be based on historical or replacement cost. Replacement cost is problematical. The depreciating asset may not be replaced. (For example, the phone company may buy fiber-optic cable for underground installations rather than new telephone poles.) It seems the responsibility of the board to allocate the surplus ($45,000 in exhibit 8) to support debt capacity, provide replacement cost to make up for inflation, or start new programs.

Some institutions may have built or retained the capacity to fund asset replacements through gifts. For them, it may not now be crucial to break even before gifts—in essence, to fund depreciation. A number of observers, however, have addressed the threats to capital formation colleges and universities may face in the future. In discussing federal policy, Anthony Knerr of Columbia University has stated, "It is not inconceivable that University endowments will have the same fate as foundations—significant restrictions on the capital formation or capital deployment." Such restrictions would presumably encourage even wealthy institutions to look to depreciation as a source of funds.

EXHIBIT 9
ABC College Building Replacement Source of Funds
(percent)

			Composite Funding Source		
Funding Source		**Building**	**Gifts**	**Depreciation**	**Debt**
Gifts	30	Academic	16.5		
Depreciation	25	and li-		13.8	
Debt	45	brary 55			24.8
Gifts	0	Organized	0		
Depreciation	55	activities		24.7	
Debt	45	and aux-			20.2
		iliary 45			
			16.5	38.5	45.0

For others, an additional depreciation or renewal charge in operations may be a major source of capital. Educational institutions aim for a capital structure that is ideal for them. Exhibit 9 presents one institution's plan for such a structure. The 45 percent debt component was the limit in one of its bond covenants. The 38.5 percent depreciation component was to be derived from setting aside 25 percent of each funded depreciation dollar (55 percent went for principal payment, the other 20 percent for ongoing renewals). Over time, the 25 percent grew with interest to the point where it could support 38 percent of the capital budget.

Where an entity employs depreciation accounting, the measure of creditworthiness is simple. Creditors and rating agencies would rate the debt capacity of an institution that keeps its books on a depreciation basis, after considering whether the institution can achieve a surplus after depreciation, rather than depleting its assets. Without generating revenue to cover its depreciation, the telephone company would have to borrow the full $1.9 million in the final year, with a corresponding drop in the equity available to support this leverage. On the other hand, creditors would judge the creditworthiness of a college that accounts on the debt-service basis on its ability to achieve 90 percent higher revenue at year 11 or a surplus during the decade. This test explains why demand is such a critical measure for agencies that rate educational institutions.

Depreciation may be viewed, then, as a way of maintaining debt capacity and so preserving the target capital structure of the college.

Under Statement of Financial Accounting Standards no. 93 and the 1973 AICPA Audit Guide for Colleges and Universities, depreciation

EXHIBIT 10
XYZ College

	Balance Sheet 6/30/85	Revenue Expense 1986	Balance Sheet 6/30/86
Unrestricted			
Current	$ 300		$ (800)
Plant	24,500	$1,000	26,400
Other	200	(details not shown)	400
	$25,000		$26,000

would be recorded in the plant fund. Only if a replacement or depreciation transfer were provided for in the operating budget would depreciation become a source of cash. Under the financial accounting concepts to be adopted in the future, however, the plant and current operating funds are likely to be combined in presenting the financial position of and changes in unrestricted net assets. If depreciation is not funded at an institution that reports under these future standards, deficiencies in sources of capital funds would become obvious.

An example from a recent set of college financial statements of a college currently combining plant and operations (XYZ College) illustrates the point (see exhibit 10).

At the beginning of the year, unrestricted funds were: current — $300,000; plant—$24.5 million; and other—$200,000. During the year, the college had a combined unrestricted surplus of $1 million. Yet, at the end of the year, the current unrestricted funds were in an $800,000 deficit. This was because the institution had advanced a net $1.9 million from working capital for plant construction.

Over the long run, this college will be unable to grow from current operations alone. Gifts and debt will be needed to supplement its internal growth capacity. A measure of that capacity is common in commercial organizations. It divides (1) the funds flow from operations, plus additions to the endowment stabilization reserve, less replacement cost depreciation, by (2) inflation-adjusted assets (see exhibit 11).[4]

In this instance, the internal growth rate is about 2 percent—hardly enough to cover the demands of renewal of physical plant at a rate that in 1986 approached 10 percent per year. The other 8 percent must come from gifts (which were not a large source of unrestricted funds to this institution in 1986) or from debt. One could expect that the institution would soon exhaust its liquidity, then its debt capacity. It would seem that a comprehensive analysis of capital structure (partic-

EXHIBIT 11
Internal Growth Capacity

$$\frac{\text{Funds Flow from Operation} + \text{Stabilization Reserve} - \text{Replacement Cost Depreciation}}{\text{Inflation-Adjusted Assets}}$$

$$\frac{1{,}000 + 800 - 1{,}700}{50{,}000}$$

2%

ularly sources of funds for physical facilities) would make sense at that institution, although it is clearly not at the danger level for debt capacity.

Danger signs would include factors such as continued enrollment decline; debt that is greater than one year's revenue, the number of dollars per student, or 5 percent of the budget; internal wrangling; decline in giving; continued expansion; and scattered creditors.[5]

Chapter 4
Choosing a Source of Funds

Before choosing a source of funds for fixed assets, student financing, and other needs, most colleges and universities have already been in, or soon plan to enter, the capital markets. Some institutions have found debt essential for well-managed survival. For others, it has provided new opportunities to improve quality and increase programs. The local commuter college, for example, whose plan is described in Exhibit 9, used debt to build dormitories, establish a national reputation, and increase enrollment. Endowed institutions have used debt to enhance their excellence, which had previously been built solely on equity, and so maintain the demand for their services.

But debt also increases risk. This risk is heightened by two operating realities of higher education—undercapitalization and overcapacity. Tax-exempt debt carries the same risk as corporate debt: Both can lead to severe financial strain through the overestimation of income available to service and repay the debt. Whether an institution has a mature debt structure or is just entering the market, effective debt management requires careful financial planning. Debt is a finite capital resource: its use consumes an implicit capital reserve and can increase future cost at the margin. While debt management is part of the capital-budgeting process, the use of debt without the capital budget or without consideration of budget constraints may result in overbuilding. Therefore, it is clear that debt raises two basic questions:

- At what point does a university's level of debt shut off the capital market?
- At what point does the marginal cost of borrowing call into question the viability of the project?

Traditionally, colleges have considered three alternatives: (1) don't build, (2) build with debt, or (3) build with cash. For some colleges, the choice is moot: The buildings are essential for survival, and there is no cash. For others whose financial position is more flexible, the choice is more real.

On a project-by-project basis, debt may not be the issue. Rather, the important choice is between building and not building, and that decision comes from a sound capital-budgeting process. The choice between debt and cash depends on the expected return on cash, the interest rate on debt, and the proportion of interest that can be recovered from a college's revenue sources. Appendix 8 contains an example of this decision.

Debt Policies

Most institutions that have debt (or are about to acquire debt) are establishing guidelines that clearly define debt policies and procedures. The first guideline is that an institution should seek the lowest overall cost of capital. Obviously, if funds are borrowed the institution wants to pay the lowest possible interest cost. If tax exempt debt costs 8 percent and the endowment earns 6 percent, it may not be responsible to borrow. But if the endowmwnt earns 12 percent, then borrowing is probably desirable.[1] A better decision criterion, however, is the return on the fixed income (debt) investments of the endowment. The portfolio managers should look upon the institution's need for capital as a potential placement of funds. In fact, these managers should be willing to accept a lower rate of return on this internal borrowing because there is no risk of default.

Second, management should balance the need for an affordable cost of capital with the desire to have each project stand on its own. In some cases, colleges have decided to incur debt only for those projects that generate incremental revenue. This will raise questions, for example, about how to build classroom debt service into the operating budget.

Third, the terms of the borrowing should match the project. Generally institutions try to match the period of the debt with the life of the project. Certainly the period of the debt should not exceed the life of the project. Few institutions, for example, would want to use long-term debt to finance equipment. Similarly, institutions want to fix interest rates that are within the project's budget. If interest rates are high and expected to decline, however, the institution may want to use short-term debt or a variable-rate debt and "fix" the interest some time in the future. The administration and the trustees must balance their willingness to accept interest rate risk with the institution's liquidity and the availability of credit support. Again, there may be a conflict between the goal of lowest possible cost and matching terms to the capital projects.

Fourth, the continuing regulatory threats to tax-exempt financing should be carefully weighed. One position to avoid is being whipsawed by short-term rates without the opportunity to "go long." Colleges should consider the convertible features of variable-debt packages available today.[2]

Fifth, the appropriation and financing decisions—and approvals—should be separate. Debt, like contributed or earned equity, should be used only to finance projects that would otherwise stand on their own.

And sixth, there should be limits set on debt exposure. Regardless of how desirable potential projects may be, institutions should not take on so much debt that it threatens institutional viability. How much debt is prudent is obviously a complicated question. Rating agencies use a variety of measures to evaluate credit risk. These may also be useful measures for internal debt capacity analyses. The ratings weight student demand heavily. Other financial considerations are also important. For a private university to maintain an A or AA rating, the criteria in exhibits 12 and 14 are typically used.

The statistics and the more complete set in appendix 5 offer a quick reference to business officers who are seeking debt. An experienced investment banker can provide guidance in interpreting and using the measures in presentations to rating agencies.

Rating agencies may consider other factors such as: liquid assets over budget expenditures; tuition dependence (more than 80 percent dependence may be considered a problem); and a good trend in state support.[3]

The data in exhibits 13 and 14 indicate that yield spreads on private college and university bonds vary substantially between rating classes.[4] The data measure the average spread in yields (84 basis points in the aggregate) between long-term college bonds and AAA-rated, tax-supported general obligations (GOs) of governmental units for private college bonds sold between 1985 and 1987. College ad university bonds with AAA-ratings carried yields that averaged 18 basis points above AAA-rated GO bonds; for AA-rated bonds, the yield was 37 basis points above the AAA-rated GO bond index. A-rated college bonds were 70 basis points higher, on average, and bonds with Baa or BBB ratings carried yields that averaged 102 basis points above AAA-rated GO bonds.

Yield spreads of this magnitude indicate the importance of achieving high credit ratings as a means of reducing the cost of capital. It is important, therefore, for colleges and universities to understand the factors that rating agencies and the market perceive as important in assessing credit strengths and weaknesses. Credit awareness is even more important in light of recent changes in bond ratings. Between 1983 and 1986, for example, Standard & Poor's Corporation down-graded 57 colleges and universities, while upgrading the ratings on

EXHIBIT 12
Measures of Creditworthiness for Private Universities

	A-Rated Issues[1]	AA-Rated Issues[2]
Student enrollment	stable	stable to increasing
Unrestricted current fund (UCF) operating surplus / UCF expenses and mandatory transfers	2%	5%
UCF accumulated surplus / UCF expenses and mandatory transfers	5%	15%
Endowment / FTE students	$15–50,000	$50,000–100,000
Admissions rate / FTE	50–70%	25–50%
Matriculation rate / FTE	20–30%	30–50%
Debt service / Operating revenues	7%	5%
Available assets / General liabilities	1X	2X
Plant equity (excluding depreciation) / Plant debt	1.1X	1.6X
Debt / Endowment	75%	50%

[1] *Source*: Survey by Boston College.
[2] *Source*: Study by Morgan Guaranty Trust Co.

only 26 institutions. (More than 50 percent of the downgradings were on public colleges and universities, and nearly all of these were associated with contemporaneous downgradings in state general obligation bond ratings.) Downgradings on private college bonds were triggered by a number of factors, including overly aggressive debt policies, poor operating results, and declining enrollments.

Controlling the Financing Process

How should the financing process be controlled? The first control is strategic planning. Questions management might ask are:

EXHIBIT 13
Yield Spreads between Private College Bonds and AAA-Rated GO Bonds

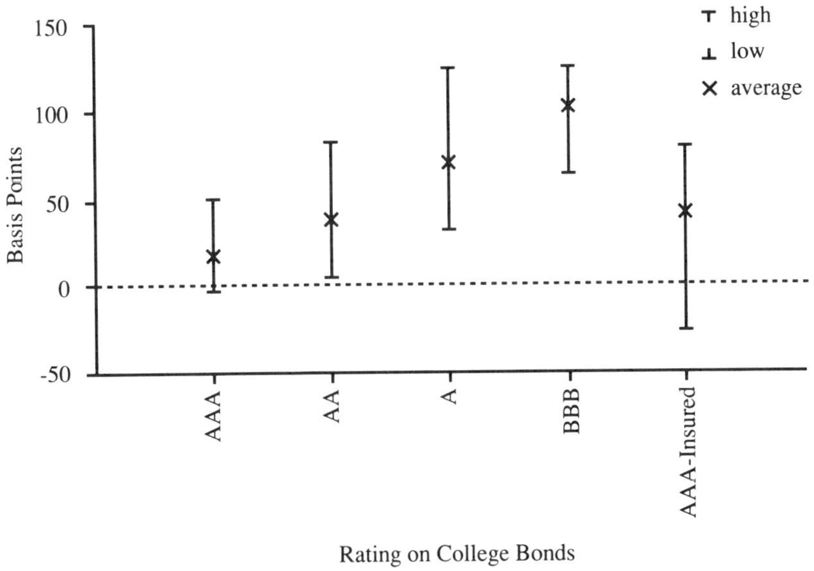

Source: Donaldson, Lufkin & Jenrette.

- What are the capital needs of the school for the next five years? The next twenty?
- What other resources (gifts, operating surpluses, endowment earnings) will be available?
- What debt will be needed to meet the gap between capital needs and available resources?
- What are the structural options? For example, can the hospital be "spun off"?
- Is there a tactical plan?
- In the long-term capital plan, how much of the capital base comes from gifts and operations? What will happen to this projection if current tax proposals are adopted? What's the ideal capital structure? The target cost of capital? How does management plan to achieve this?
- How tight is the operating budget? Can it sustain more debt service? Is management prepared to manage a construction program—including bonding, retention, insurance, bidding and oversight?
- Capital financing should not focus solely on facilities, but should also address student financing. In this case, what is ideal capital structure?

EXHIBIT 14
Selected Credit Characteristics of Private College Bond Ratings

	Average by Rating Class (Standard & Poor's Rating)				
Characteristic	**AAA**	**AA**	**A**	**BBB**	**AAA-Insured**
Selectivity ratio	24.6%	39.1%	57.8%	74.2%	62.3%
Matriculation ratio	55.9%	46.7%	41.5%	57.2%	44.0%
Tuition as percent of current revenue	29.6%	47.3%	65.2%	62.7%	52.2%
Unrestricted assets/current expenditures	.80	.92	.42	.33	.34
Endowment per student ($000s)	$141	$65	$14	$5	$12
Debt/endowment	.19	.35	1.43	3.00	1.16

Data based on sample of 39 private college bonds.
Unrestricted assets = fund balance in unrestricted current fund and quasi-endowment fund balance.
Current revenue = total revenue in unrestricted current fund.
Source: Donaldson, Lufkin & Jenrette.

Another aspect of control to be considered is operations after the debt is issued. Management should ask:

- Does the financial organization have the resources to manage the details of debt accounting?
- Is there a formal understanding of how to comply with bond indentures?
- How will it ensure that spending on each project will approximate the projected drawdown schedule?
- How will it make certain that overspenders do not drain the whole construction fund (or other restricted capital funds)?
- Is it prepared to plan and oversee the securities invested with the trustees?
- What is done to prevent collateral and interest-rate exposures with repurchase agreements such as the ones that befell those who dealt securities forms like ESM, Lombard Wall, or Lion Capital?
- Is the trustee constantly rolling over short-term investments if the yield curve is steep?

EXHIBIT 15
Funding Structure

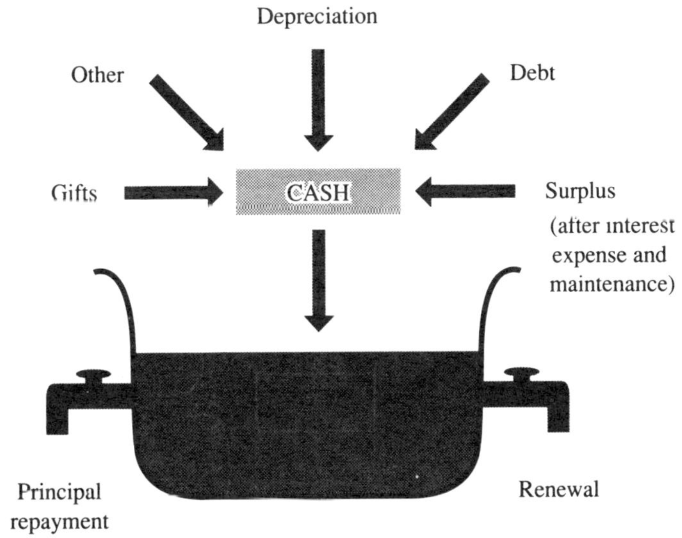

Source: John R. Smith, Boston College.

Blended Pool of Funds

The current emphasis on university credit ratings suggests that college treasurers are more likely to be concerned with debt as it affects the institution as a whole than to consider it on a project-by-project basis. In the example in exhibit 9, the institution expected that debt would represent 45 percent of its overall plant capital. This is the way corporations view their capital structure. With an overall capital plan, the college can build with both debt and cash. Though laws may restrict borrowing to specific buildings and gifts to others, business officers really seek to fund capital projects from a blended revolving pool that includes both. Asset lives and interest rates, to the extent permitted under the bond indentures, will be uncoupled from the external debt.

In 1975, in connection with a bond issue that at the time was the largest one ABC College had issued, a structure was established for funding future projects (see exhibit 15). Cash from various sources (debt, gifts, a funded facilities-use charge, and the operating surplus after interest expense and maintenance) was moved to the unexpended plant fund. In turn, this pool of money was tapped for principal

EXHIBIT 16
Components of Typical Bond Issue

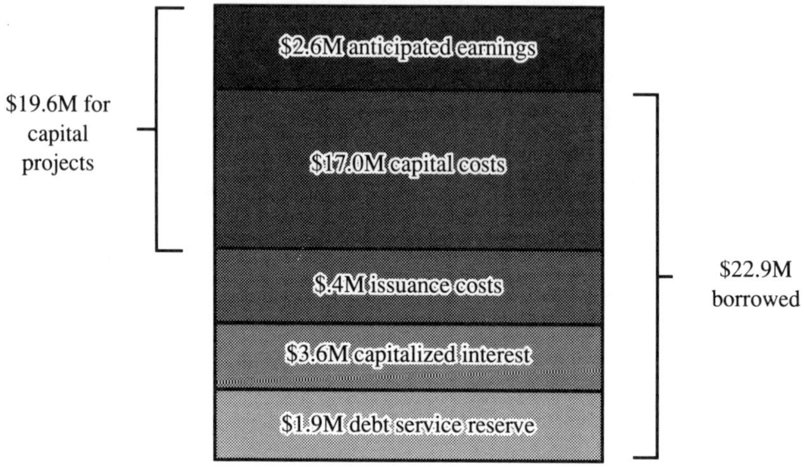

repayment, renewal, and additional building. Obviously, the first step in establishing such a model is to identify capital project priorities. Then the college must identify and project various funding sources over a 25-year future period. At many universities the next question would be, what do we charge the departments?

In order to answer this question, it is necessary to analyze the costs and benefits of the components of funding, as from a debt issue, over their life cycles. The components of a typical pre-1987 bond issue is shown in exhibit 16. In this case, the colleges borrowed $22.9 million for $19.6 million of capital projects. Each of these components is a source of funds or a use of funds to the college, and therefore to its various departments. Assume, further, that portfolio performance enabled the college to add $20 million of its own funds (perhaps by designation of quasi-endowment) to the bond issue.

In the example shown in exhibit 17, almost $40 million would be available for capital projects. In this example, the $20 million of internal funds are already supporting an activity at the college, so earnings on them during the construction period are not available for building. Furthermore, over the life of the capital project, the college must return to the endowment an amount that supports these operations. In essence, the college has borrowed from endowment users as well as from bondholders.

Issuance, remarketing, and other costs must be charged to the departments or the buildings, but a debt service reserve and earnings on the debt service reserve are available to liquidate the bond issue at

EXHIBIT 17
Blended Pool Components

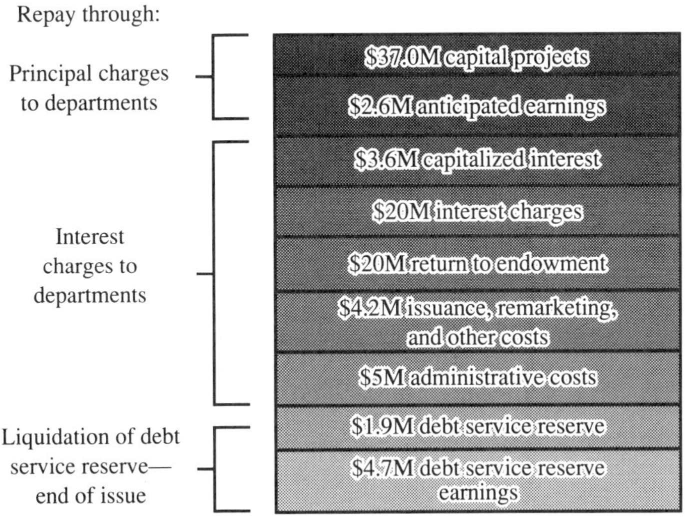

its termination. Exhibit 16 shows the effect of analyzing each of these components: Some are repaid through principal charges to the departments, some through interest, and those related to debt service reserves, at the end of the issue. It would make good sense for business officers establishing a blended pool to explain the nature and size of these charges in some detail to the departments that will be paying for them.

Once the costs and benefits of these funding components are analyzed, management must establish policies to account for each of them. The amount that is returned to the endowment each year may be related to an external borrowing rate, the total return on the endowment, or the endowment spending rate. An investment in facilities in any environment is unlikely to generate the sort of return pattern (up 25 percent one year, down 15 percent the next) that is experienced by the endowment as a whole. A return of simply the spending rate would penalize the funds: At the end of the project period, the endowment fund would not have grown.

Therefore, some institutions have chosen a fixed income return to the endowment. (This return varies in practice, however, because departments are gaining access to a blended pool at an interest rate that depends neither on the debt component nor the internal funds component, but the asset life.) The repayment period for each department can be set on what it can afford, but should be related to the life of the component asset—three to five years for computers, perhaps

EXHIBIT 18
Blended Pool Policies

Policy Choice	Example
Return to endowment	T-Bill plus 2 percent
Repayment period	Asset component life
Issuance and remarketing costs	Add to effective interest rate
Project criteria	Dollar limits by department
Base for allocating • Capitalized interest • Anticipated earnings	Estimated drawdown schedule
Substitution of projects	With approval
Interest rate	Tied to asset life
External reporting	Column for "bank"

EXHIBIT 19
Capital Cost Allocation Model

Establish capital-project priorities
Identify funding sources
Analyze costs and benefits of funding components over their life cycle
Set project pool policies
Allocate costs/charge departments
Manage pool

25 to 30 years for buildings. The criteria for including projects in the pool depends to some extent on restrictions set forth in the bond indentures, but in any case should include dollar limits by department.

The actual allocation of costs and benefits, particularly capitalized interest and anticipated earnings on construction funds, is complex. These elements could be allocated on a monthly proportion of costs invested in each particular capital project to the total invested to date, or they could be charged on an estimated drawdown schedule. If departmental operations are charged amounts that differ from external debt, this must be accommodated in financial reporting for the institution as a whole. Exhibit 18 displays blended pool policies set forth by one institution.

Finally, after policies have been set, the financial department must allocate the costs and charge departments according to these policies, and the controller's staff and the treasurer's staff must jointly manage the assets and liabilities of the blended pool. Each of these steps fits into the total capital cost allocation model (see exhibit 19).

Chapter 5
Credit Support

As discussed previously, a number of fixed income vehicles were created in the 1980s to lower the cost of money through short-term instruments. These techniques included refunding measures and other structures that exploited market efficiencies for the benefit of the issuer. The use of bond insurance and letters of credit or lines of credit grew as purchasers of debt sought to substitute financial guarantees for institutional credit. According to a leading investment bank, this has, to some extent, "been occasioned by a crowded and dynamic marketplace where neither the debt purchaser nor the rating services have had adequate time to examine each credit."[1]

Insured bonds typically sell at yields that average 60 basis points lower than BBB-rated colleges and 30 points below A-rated bonds (see exhibit 12).

Currently five companies provide insurance on debt issued by colleges and universities. All have received triple-A ratings from Standard & Poor's. In 1986, Moody's Investor Services agreed to rate two of the insurers, "MBIA" and "FGIC," triple A and to consider other insured issues for ratings on a case-by-case basis. Although triple-A rated bonds are the highest credit quality and command the lowest rates in the tax-exempt bond market, insurance is not always the most cost-effective method of reducing financing expense. Market conditions in all cases may not provide an interest-rate differential between an uninsured and an insured bond issue that is sufficient to cover the cost of the insurance.

One positive development to come out of the congressional session that produced the Tax Reform Act was the authorization of the creation of the College Construction Loan Insurance Association (an independent corporation to be owned jointly by the government, the higher education institutions, Sally Mae, and the general public). This new insurer (known as CCLI or "CLIA") is authorized to insure and reinsure college and university loans, to give letters of credit, and to make direct loans. The corporation is mandated to do a significant percentage of business over time with institutions that have lower credit ratings.

The provisions of the reauthorization act that established CLIA should provide assistance to a large group of institutions that at present and historically have had little or no access to the capital markets. Observers of the market for college credit anticipate that CLIA will serve primarily two-year public institutions and those liberal arts and other four-year private institutions that do not have an endowment to support an investment grade rating (or, consequently, cannot otherwise attract credit support that would provide a triple-A rating).

This market has a number of needs: First, as two-year institutions look beyond traditional commuter markets, they may have a need for residence halls. Second, some institutions are expanding with gyms and student unions, and many have an immediate demand for telecommunication systems and computers. Finally, there is a market for most institutions to renew the space built during the late 1950s and 1960s, when colleges were expanding to meet student demands. As discussed previously, this space has reached a point where perhaps 20 percent is unsatisfactory. A great deal of money may be needed to renew this space, and CLIA can provide credit support for some of these funds.

As this book was being prepared, CLIA was in the process of obtaining licenses to sell credit insurance in the various states, planning to raise capital from both the federal government and private investors, preparing financial plans in order to obtain ratings from the rating agencies, and establishing underwriting criteria and administrative systems to operate in the future.

Chapter 6
The Effect of the Tax Reform Act

The signing of the Tax Reform Act of 1986 heralded the most comprehensive change in the tax-exempt market in 20 years. This legislation introduced major constraints on the future supply of new tax-exempt debt and changed the demand by investors for tax-exempt income. These effects together have already altered the shape of the tax-exempt yield curve and added to the volatility of tax-exempt interest rates. In addition, this legislation changed accepted methods for structuring and marketing new debt issues.

Tax Reform and Its Impact on Supply and Demand

The Tax Reform Act of 1986 reduced the overall supply of new issues in several ways: It tightened the definition of governmental purpose and sharpened the distinction between government purpose and private activity; it removed the tax-exempt financing eligibility for some private activity bonds; and it placed most other private activity bonds under restrictive annual volume limits. The list of no longer exempt private activity bonds includes industrial development bonds (IDBs) for pollution control; sports, convention, and trade show facilities; parking facilities; industrial parks; and hydroelectric generating facilities.

Most other private activity bonds, including student loan bonds, are subject to a new and unified state volume cap. Prior law had established two volume caps. Student loan bonds and most IDBs were limited on a state-by-state basis to the greater of $150 per capita or $200 million, while single-family mortgage revenue bonds were limited to $200

Ed. note: The bulk of the material in this chapter was taken, with permission, from the text of two speeches: "Financing Higher Education: Life after Tax Reform," presentation given by Diana Taylor, senior vice president, Donaldson, Lufkin & Jenrette, at the NACUBO Annual Meeting, July 1987; and "What's New in Debt Financing in Higher Education," presentation given by David C. Clapp at the Symposium on New Ideas in Capital Financing, sponsored by the Forum for College Financing Alternatives, October 20, 1986.

million or 9 percent of mortgage originations. Other private activity bonds, such as multifamily rental bonds, were not subject to volume limits. Under Tax Reform, all private activity bonds are subject to a single volume cap, with the important exceptions of nonprofit institutions, such as colleges and universities, and governmentally owned airports, docks, wharves, and solid waste disposal facilities. The new unified volume limits are $75 per capita or $250 million (whichever is greater) in 1987 and $50 per capita or $150 million after 1987. The impact of these constraints is substantial. Average monthly new issue volume in the first four months of 1987—$10.4 billion—was 24 percent below average volume in 1986 and 44 percent below 1985 volume.[1]

Higher education emerged from these supply side constraints relatively unscathed. Public and private colleges and universities were not included under the unified volume ceilings. However, Tax Reform did impose a limit of $150 million per institution on tax-exempt nonhospital debt of private institutions. This has effectively barred several large private universities from future market access (excluding specific projects permitted under a transition period). Unfortunately, this institutional ceiling has driven an artificial wedge between the cost of capital for large private institutions and other higher education institutions at a time when all universities are concerned with controlling costs.

The most significant impact of tax reform on the demand side, which is composed of investors' demand for tax-exempt products, is the general reduction in marginal tax rates. For individuals, the top marginal rate has been cut from 50 percent in 1986 to 38.5 percent in 1987 and 28 percent thereafter. For corporations, the top marginal rate has been reduced from 46 percent in 1986 to 40 percent in 1987 and 34 percent after 1987. Corporations are also subject to stiffened rules for determining income that that is subject to an alternative minimum tax (AMT). These new rules require tax-exempt income on governmental purpose bonds and nonprofit entity bonds to be counted as excess book income subject to AMT; and tax-exempt interest on all other private activity bonds is required to be counted as preference income, which is also subject to the AMT. Therefore, in order to be attractive to the investing public, tax-exempt bonds must carry a yield closer to the taxable yield available in the market.

In what is perhaps the most significant change for corporate investors, the Tax Reform Act of 1986 removed an important incentive for commercial bank investment in tax-exempts. Prior to Tax Reform, banks were allowed to deduct from their taxable income 80 percent of the interest cost on funds used to buy tax-exempts. This interest deductibility provided banks with opportunities to buy tax-exempts as long as the yield was greater than their after-tax cost of funds. Tax reform removed this interest deductibility except for qualified small issues, defined as governmental purpose bonds or nonprofit entity bonds where the borrowing entity issues less than $10 million in total volume per year. As a result, banks will generally find tax-exempts of interest only when the yield on them is greater than the *before-tax* cost of funds. The removal of interest deductibility, effective for tax-exempts purchased after August 1986, has seriously eroded bank demand. Large banks, which report weekly to the Federal Reserve System, held $61.5 billion in tax-exempts at the end of 1985; by December 1986, their holdings had declined to $54.6 billion, and, through early 1987, an additional $3 billion was liquidated. Holdings of short-term tax-exempts declined by $2.9 billion, or 27 percent, between 1985 and 1986. As discussed later, the absence of bank demand has important consequences for the shape of the tax-exempt yield curve and its volatility.

The Effect of Tax Reform on the Structure and Marketing of Tax-Exempt Bonds

The principal attraction of the tax-exempt market to colleges and universities has historically been its lower cost of capital. Tax Reform has drastically curtailed arbitrage benefits available to issuers of tax-exempt securities. The overriding rule now is that issuers must rebate any arbitrage to the federal government. Generally, arbitrage not subject to rebate is now permitted only for a six-month period after sale and then only if substantially all bond proceeds have been expended for the purpose of the borrowing. Debt service reserve funds are considered "nonpurpose" investments; therefore, bond issues structured with reserve funds are not permitted a six-month temporary period to earn unlimited yields, under present interpretations. Debt service reserve funds are limited generally to 10 percent of bond proceeds, unless prior bond indentures require larger reserve funds. Colleges and universities are permitted to collateralize bond issues with larger reserve funds, but, as with all tax-exempt issuers, the earnings rate on such funds is limited to the bond issue yield. If funds are invested at a yield higher than the rate on the bond issue, that money must be rebated to the federal government. In addition, the bond issue yield used to determine the limit on investment earnings must now be calculated based on the gross proceeds of debt sale, without allowance for any costs of issuance other than credit enhancement fees. This measure of yield further reduces the earnings permitted on investments. Under the new rules, issuers must keep records on an issue-by-issue basis and rebate any arbitrage profits to the U.S. Treasury every five years.

The rules regarding advance refundings were also changed. In general, new issues sold after January 1986 are allowed to be advance refunded only one time. Private activity bonds, including private college and university bonds, are also subject to added restrictions on the use of bond proceeds. In particular, no more than 2 percent of the proceeds from debt sales can be used to finance various costs of issuance. Included as examples of these costs are:

- underwriting spreads,
- legal fees, including counsel for issuers and underwriters,
- financial advisory fees,
- rating agency fees,
- trustee and paying agent fees,
- fees for accounting services required for a debt issue, and
- fees for special feasibility studies necessary for the sale of new debt.

The Choice between Variable-Rate and Fixed-Rate Bonds

In this new environment, long-term capital planning is critical for the implementation of successful debt management strategies. One of the most important elements of that process must be flexibility in the management of new and outstanding debt. Recent moves in tax-exempt yields suggest that tax reform may have contributed to increased market volatility. For example, the Bond Buyer Revenue Bond Index (RBI) jumped from 7.08 percent in mid-March 1987 to 8.32 percent in late May, an increase of 124 basis points. By contrast, Treasury yields increased by only 117 basis points in the same period. Many market observers attribute the higher volatility of tax-exempts to the absence of bank demand. Regardless of the cause, this volatility emphasizes the need for flexible debt management strategies. The introduction of a "capacity constraint" of $150 million on the exempt debt of private institutions also requires careful planning. While most colleges are well below this limit, others are uncomfortably close, and major capital projects could quickly exhaust the capacity remaining under the ceiling. Detailed capital plans help educational institutions to structure and time their new tax-exempt issues appropriately; in some cases, it may even be appropriate to reserve future tax-exempt capacity by first tapping the taxable market.

The new rules imposed by the Tax Reform Act of 1986 have complicated the analysis of risks and benefits between variable-rate debt and long-term fixed-rate bonds. At present, many colleges and universities have converted earlier variable-rate issues to a longer-term fixed-rate mode. Long rates are still moderate and fixed-rate debt does provide a cap on future debt service expenses. Moreover, the recent surge in volatility suggests that financial markets are unusually uncertain over the course of future rates. For risk-averse borrowers, long-term financing may be the strategy of choice to avoid the consequences of sharp and sudden increases in rates; all decisions will have to be made within the context of prevailing market conditions.

Offsetting these benefits to long-term financing, however, is the negative arbitrage under the new temporary period rules. Formerly, an appropriate measure of temporary period arbitrage was the comparison of long-term tax-exempt yields with three-year Treasury yields. As noted in exhibit 20, this spread (the "US3-TE30" spread) produced potential temporary period profits as high as 300 basis points for A-rated issuers. By contrast, the US3-TE30 spread averaged a negative 37 basis points through May 1987. More relevant under the new rules is the spread between six-month Treasury yields and long-term tax exempts (the US6-TE30 spread). As the exhibit points out, this spread turned negative in 1982 and averaged a negative 127 basis points through May 1987.

Variable-rate debt financings, on the other hand, can still be invested to earn and keep positive arbitrage under the six-month rules. The spread on six-month notes has averaged more than 150 basis points in 1987. Based on recent average underwriting spreads of $15 per $1,000 par value, temporary period arbitrage of 150 basis points can recover nearly half of these costs. Moreover, the tax-exempt yield curve remained steeply sloped: The RBI, at 8.32 percent in late May 1987, was 394 basis points above the six-month note rate. At maturity differentials this wide, issuers should give serious consideration to variable-rate debt.

Asset/Liability Management: Caps, Swaps, and Self-Insuring Interest Rate Risk

Many colleges and universities have sufficient resources to develop self-insurance programs as a way of hedging the interest rate risks on variable-rate debt. These resources—current operating fund surpluses

EXHIBIT 20
Arbitrage Yield
Spreads in the Tax-Exempt Market

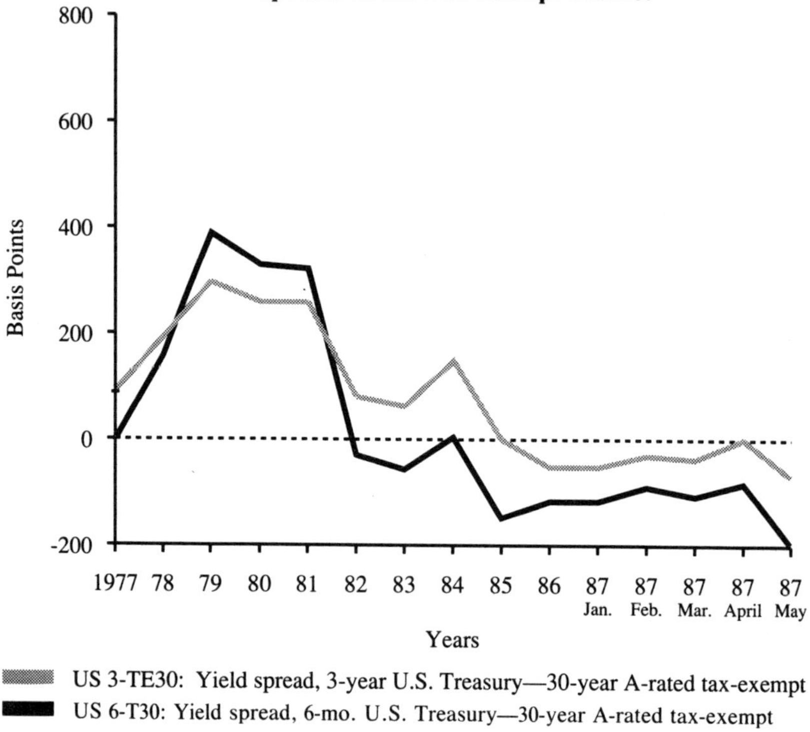

Source: Donaldson, Lufkin & Jenrette.

or unrestricted endowment fund assets—can be employed to reduce or eliminate the cash flow risk from sudden interest rate surges. The objective is to structure a portion of these assets so that the return on them mirrors the interest rate sensitivity of liabilities. Expressed another way, this type of asset/liability matching attempts to achieve strong positive correlations between total asset returns and debt service costs, a strategy similar to the duration matching strategies commonly employed by bank or pension fund management. In this context, it is irrelevant that past endowment portfolio returns have often appeared to be negatively correlated with changes in tax-exempt rates. Asset returns dropped in 1982 and 1984—periods when tax-exempt rates rose.

As a result of this market uncertainty, other interest rate insurance vehicles are beginning to develop—among these, a market in interest rate cap agreements that effectively cap future costs. Under an interest rate cap agreement, the seller (intermediary) agrees to pay the buyer (variable rate borrower) the difference between an agreed-upon index of variable rates and the negotiated interest rate ceiling. In the current market context, for example, a cap might be negotiated at 8.32 percent. During the life of the agreement (which generally does not exceed ten years), the seller agrees to pay the buyer the difference whenever the index exceeds the 8.32 percent cap.

The cost of the cap to the buyer is an up-front fee. It is important, therefore, to assess the cost of this insurance relative to its potential benefit, which requires a present value analysis of the expected savings over the life of the agreement.[2]

An interest rate swap, on the other hand, is a contract between two counterparties that involves payments by each side to its counterparty. Payments are calculated as an interest rate applied to a national principal amount with a fixed rate set at execution. The floating rate index is specified at execution and is reset periodically on dates specified in the contract, and payments are often made on a net basis. Swaps will become increasingly important to traditional tax-exempt financings as issuers attempt to mitigate insufficient investments.

An interest rate swap is not an exchange of debt. There is no assumption by one party of another party's liability. It is simply a set of cash flows that dovetail with existing liabilities. Neither are interest rate swaps securities. There are no requirements for SEC registration, prospectus, due diligence, or margin. Swaps are not easily arranged for weak (sub-BBB) or project credits. If an institution has already pledged its revenues and cannot pledge assets, management may find no willing swap counterparties. It is also not a long-term market; generally, ten years is the maximum. Furthermore, swaps are not easily used to hedge precise principal amortization. Swaps are usually against bullet national amounts of $25 million or more in two, three, five, seven, or ten years. Amortizing swaps do exist, but they are expensive. Swaps are not tax-exempt instruments: the swap flows themselves are taxable to any taxpaying entity.

Swaps are proving increasingly attractive to issuers because they afford a hedge to offset fixed-rate debt cash flows with variable-rate payments and variable-rate debt with fixed-rate payments. The swap market allows sophisticated issuers to:

- capture arbitrage opportunities to the extent permissible resulting from market imperfections,
- avoid regulatory and tax constraints,
- arbitrate international or interstate tax law differences, and
- exploit different credit premiums in different parts of the yield curve.

There are, however, several major obstacles to participating in interest rate swaps for traditional tax-exempt borrowers. These include the fact that most bond counsel do not understand swap transactions, and, even if they do, they often do not approve them. The authority to enter into a swap is virtually never specifically given to municipal issuers. Often, swaps will require new legislation. If an issuer does not get new legislation, it will require a difficult opinion of counsel. Finally, security is a difficult issue. Revenues often are already pledged for outstanding debt. If so, is there anything else left to pledge?[3]

Timing, Call Options, and Refunding Strategies

Under the old rules, borrowers were insulated from the full impact of cyclical peaks in interest rates by the arbitrage profits legally available. Tax-exempt borrowers also had incentives to carry out planned new issues knowing that any future declines in interest rates could produce immediate debt service savings through advance refundings. The new rules restrict these practices and increase the potential cost of poor market timing.

Market timing is also vital if issuers are to maximize the present value savings from advance refundings. These savings are determined by the relationship between current tax-exempt rates and rates on the old bonds, and by the relationship between tax-exempt rates on refunding bonds and maximum rates allowed on escrow fund investments. Current arbitrage rules limit the yield on escrow fund investments to the lower of the true interest cost (TIC) on the refunding bonds or the posted rate on the Treasury special State and Local Government Series (SLUGS) securities.

The yield spread between seven-year Treasuries and the Bond Buyer Revenue Bond Index has been volatile, swinging from positive to negative in 1987 (see exhibit 21). Negative spreads, of course, reduce the savings from advance refundings. By establishing a target level of savings in advance, issuers can be prepared to quickly refund when conditions are most favorable.

Prior to the Tax Reform Act of 1986, colleges and universities were not limited in the number of times they could advance refund a given issue. As a result, they were encouraged to advance refund early and often whenever savings could be realized. Indeed, many higher education bonds sold in 1984 and 1985, and callable in 1994 and 1995, have been advance refunded with new debt maturities often extended beyond the life of the original bonds. Under the new rules, new issues sold after January 1986 can be advance refunded only once. Moreover,

EXHIBIT 21
Refunding Yield Spreads, Seven-Year U.S. Treasury versus RBI

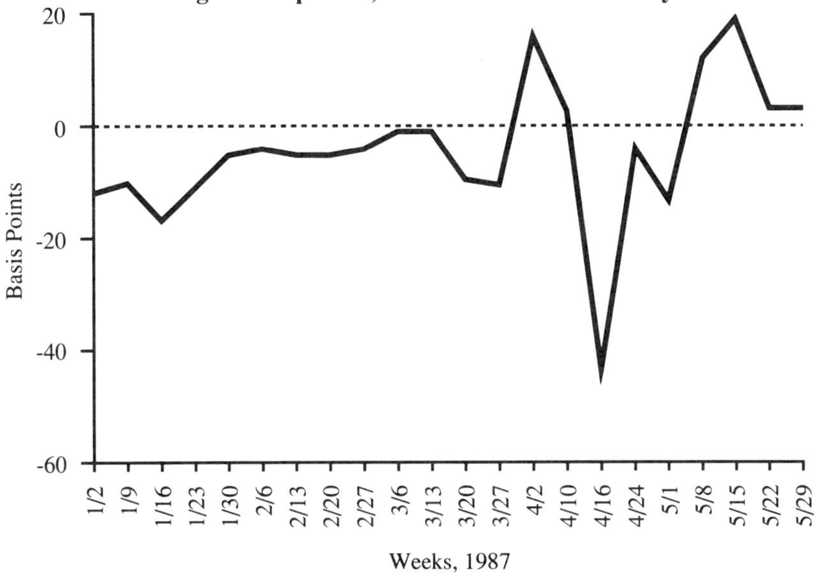

Yield spread: Yield on seven-year maturity U.S. Treasury notes minus yield on Bond Buyer Revenue Bond Index.

Source: Donaldson, Lufkin & Jenrette.

the life of refunding bonds cannot be extended beyond 120 percent of the weighted average economic life of the facilities originally financed. These new restrictions should cause colleges and universities to reevaluate the traditional rules of thumb used to time advance refundings and to reassess the standard package of optional redemption features on bond issues.

In the past, a decision to advance refund was often made based on a target level of present value savings that could be achieved, for example, 5 percent of the original par value. Under the new rules, which allow only one advance refunding for any bonds issued after August 1986, issuers must consider this threshold savings level more carefully, as a decision to refund in one time period forecloses the opportunity to exercise the option in a later period, when interest rates may be even lower.

The new limit on advance refunding also calls into question the traditional package of call option features. The conventional package—a ten-year deferred call with a premium of 2 or 3 percent—is no longer as valuable now that it can be exercised only once. One alternative is to shorten the period of call deferment on new issues from the standard ten years to five or seven years. Depending on investors' expectations regarding future interest rates, the added call premium may be more than offset by the flexibility offered for current refundings, which are not restricted by tax reform.

New bond issues may also be structured with extendible call options. Under this scenario, an issuer could structure new debt with a relatively short initial call period of, for instance, five years. The issuer would reserve the right to extend the call period at a subsequent date and to set a price to be paid by investors for the extended call protection. Investors would have the option of paying the fee and being assured of an added call protection period at the original bond rate or facing the risk that their bonds would be called at the first refunding date. Since the presence of a call option constrains the appreciation potential on high coupon bonds in low interest rate environments, the announcement of an extended call deferment would result in an immediate price appreciation for investors. By selling the extended call, borrowers could realize immediate cash savings without jeopardizing the subsequent use of an advance refunding.[4]

Taxable Financing Alternatives

With the enactment of the tax bill of 1986, colleges and universities, both public and private, will be looking toward different financing vehicles to meet their capital requirements. Although a substantial portion of these requirements will be met through the issuance of tax-exempt bonds, issuers will need to evaluate taxable financing as well. In fact, sales of taxable bonds by local governments and authorities are leaving the realm of imagination and becoming reality. Inasmuch as the new federal tax bill, which prohibits tax-exempt financing for some kinds of projects, imposes stricter volume limits for higher education and requires issuers to rebate to the Treasury any net interest earnings resulting from bond sales, taxable financing alternatives may prove more desirable from management's standpoint and, in some situations, may be the only alternative. According to a nine-month compilation of issuing activity in the municipal bond market prepared by IDD Information Services/PSA Municipal Data Base, approximately 206 issues of local government bonds totaling $2.17 billion were sold in taxable form (meaning that interest payments are subject to federal income tax) through October 1986. During 1985 a total of only $300 million of such issues were sold, almost all of which were by one issuer. It is clear that even though interest rates are higher on taxable financings than for traditional tax-exempt bonds, which are exempt from interest payments, there are some situations where it may be the most appropriate vehicle.

Chief among the taxable financing alternatives available for higher education issues are 1) taxable commercial paper, 2) medium-term notes, 3) U.S. public securities, 4) private placements, and 5) Eurodollar bonds. In addition, higher education issuers may become more interested in participating in hedging techniques such as interest rate swaps; and, although the $2.17 billion taxable financings for the nine months of 1986 pale in comparison to the $104.6 billion of financings done on a tax-exempt basis, it is clear that activity in taxable bonds is on the increase. It is too early to ascertain exactly which type of taxable security will be most favorable for issuers. Just which taxable instruments will be most favorable will depend on how the rate relationships between taxable and tax-exempt instruments develop.[5] Appendix 6 summarizes both taxable and tax-exempt financings.

As this goes to press, it is not clear how clarifications and regulations related to the Tax Reform Act will affect borrowings of colleges and universities, beyond the rules described above. Although the changes to the arbitrage regulations appear to have a great effect on colleges and universities already, the restrictions are not as great under the Tax Reform Act as they could have been. It is always possible that Congress may revise its position on college and university debt as it seeks additional revenue in the future. For example, colleges could become subject to statewide per capita limits that now affect student loan authorities and industrial financing agencies. In addition, it is possible that tax-exempt interest on college obligations could be subject to the alternative minimum tax.

According to David Clapp,"Other sources for debt financing will doubtless become available. The foreign market is still relatively untapped [although there has been some activity]. The main trouble with that market until now is that it has required big issues (to get attention) and short amortization. Some other devices, such as tuition fee futures, may begin to find acceptance as time goes on. College and university financings occupy a reasonably good niche in the debt markets. The default and late payment records are excellent, better than the statistics for housing and health care. The defaults that have occurred have received attention to some extent because of their infrequency. But the higher education coalition should not lose sight of the fact that the environment for capital financing is not as good as it has been in the past. The lack of federal support is documented. The fact that colleges and universities are in a competitive environment at a time when costs are rising faster than the ability to increase revenues is not lost on investors. It seems that the devices to finance are there but that ability to access those devices is far from certain. Many institutions are already leveraged and, on average, their financing needs do not attract the same attention as do larger issues. Using credit enhancement, creating pools for financing, and making use of state authority programs (in the states where they are available) seem worthy of increased attention."[6]

Chapter 7

Accounting Issues over the Life Cycle of Debt

Most of the principles of fund accounting were developed before colleges incurred significant amounts of debt. To take one example, debt is currently not recognized as a source of funds on the statement of changes in fund balances. Any borrowing generates a number of accounting transactions throughout its life cycle, including capitalization of interest, extinguishment, hedging, and recovery of interest costs from federal sponsors. Business officers will find that, at one time or another, an issue of plant debt affects each of the four subgroups in the plant fund. Initially, the proceeds and debt reside in the unexpended plant fund subgroup; after construction is complete, the assets and the debt belong in the invested-in-plant subgroup. Depending on the terms of the debt, reserves may be required for renewal and replacement and for debt service as well. Sample accounting entries for the life cycle of debt are shown in appendix 1.

Premiums, Discounts, and Costs of Issuance

At the closing, debt may be sold at a premium or discount and a university will probably incur legal, printing, distribution, and other costs connected with its issue. Often these costs are paid for from the bond proceeds, though they may come from internal sources as well. While bond discounts do not have all the characteristics of assets, they are often separately accounted for as such, so as to separate transactions in these accounts from the amount of outstanding debt, which is generally reported broadly in the financial statements of the institution.

In theory, issuance costs are an addition to the effective interest rate of the debt throughout its life and should be amortized in such a way as to keep interest level throughout. This treatment is most common for zero coupon and other deep discount debt. In practice, however, most institutions amortize issuance costs and nominal discounts and premiums in a way that is both easy to calculate and that approximates the effective interest method—most often the straight-line method or, for debt with serial maturities, the principal outstanding method. Original issuance costs are most frequently amortized over the stated (long-term) maturity of a variable-rate debt issue, while periodic marketing expenses are not capitalized but are treated as expenditures of the remarketing period (typically a year or less). In some cases, a university may combine expenses related to a short-term (bridge) issue with those on a subsequent longer-run financing, if both are part of a single financing plan.

Where the debt structure is frequently revised, it may be necessary to determine the period benefited by each type of issuance cost (to "componentize" it) and to amortize each portion of issuance cost over the debt outstanding in that period. For example, the legal costs of structuring a set of documents may not be repeated with a remarketing or reissue, though an institution may incur additional costs of printing the documents, as well as the debt instruments themselves, at the time of each reissuance. In any instance, the amortization of costs of issuance should be treated as part of the mandatory transfer for debt service in current funds expenditures. Exhibit 22 shows one of many alternatives for componentizing issuance costs.

Debt Service Reserves

A second feature of tax-exempt debt is the establishment of debt service reserves. At the time of issue, these reserves, together with the related debt, are normally entered in the retirement of indebtedness subgroup, together with the issuance costs discussed above. Interest earned on these reserves is accounted for in various ways, depending on the terms of the borrowing. In some cases, it may be treated as an addition to the plant funds; if so, it is available to reduce the mandatory debt service transfer from current or other funds. In other cases, the balance may accumulate with interest in the reserve fund, without a corresponding reduction in the mandatory transfer. In both of these instances, the debt service reserve would be used to make the final payments on a debt issue. At that time, investments in the reserve fund, together with the related debt, would be removed from the balance sheet. Other debt agreements may call for the retirement of bonds with debt service reserve balances.

EXHIBIT 22
Componentized Issuance Costs

	1 year (expense)	5 year (conversion)	30 years
Underwriting			x
Lawyer		x	
Official statement		x	
Discount			x
Accounting		x	
Certificates		x	
Remarketing	x		

Allocation of Debt Service among Projects

Particularly with the relatively recent requirement to capitalize interest, many institutions now allocate debt service to benefiting departments or schools. This allocation is made on the basis of a comparison of specific project costs to total project costs, most frequently from the original budget of the issue, though actual expenditures are also used as a basis.

Treatment of Construction in Process

Institutions have employed two methods, equally acceptable, to account for the transfer of construction costs, as well as the related debt, from the unexpended-plant-funds subgroup to funds invested in plant. Institutions using the first method make the transfer as construction costs are incurred; the rest account for work in progress within the unexpended-plant-funds subgroup throughout the construction period and transfer the amounts to the invested-in-plant subgroup when work is done.

Other

The introduction of depreciation to college and university financial statements has had little effect on accounting for debt. The major issue arises when the asset and debt have different lives. In all cases, each should be accounted for separately.

EXHIBIT 23
Volume of Fixed-Rate Securities vs. Variable-Rate Securities in Higher Education Financing
1982–September 1986

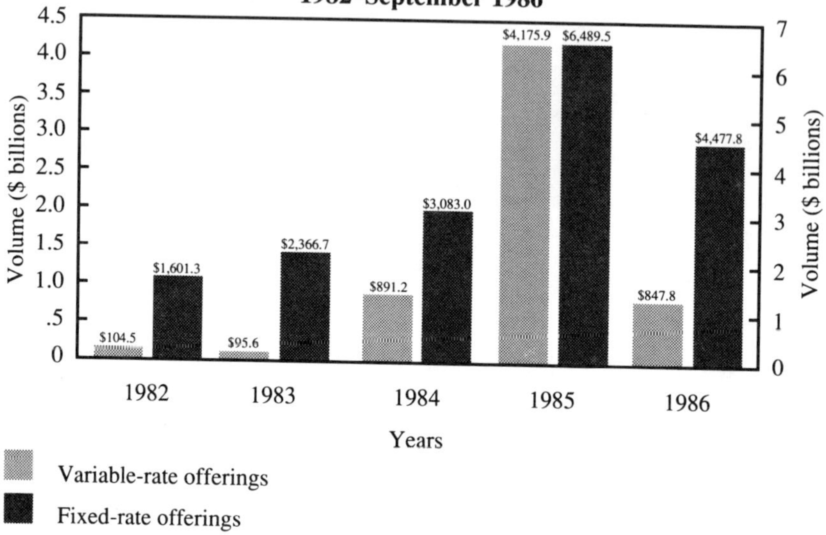

Source: Information Services, Inc.

Life Cycle Considerations

Recently many colleges and universities have issued short-term debt that can be converted into long-term obligations (see exhibit 23). The interest rate while the debt has a short-term form does not necessarily represent the rate expected over the long term. Furthermore, the institutions' obligation for debt service at the end of the issue is met through funded debt service reserves. Some have proposed that debt service could appropriately be leveled in these circumstances at a rate that is expected over the life cycle of the long-term issue (see exhibit 24). They cite precedents in (1) the straight-line treatment of operating leases with escalation clauses and (2) the use of an average interest rate based on the estimated term of debt that is issued with stated increases in the rate at specific intervals.

Such treatment may be appropriate for internal capital management; that is, a long-term project that is feasible only at (lower) current short-term rates should be forced to justify itself over the long term. It may not be appropriate for external financial reporting, however, because

EXHIBIT 24
Debt Life Cycle

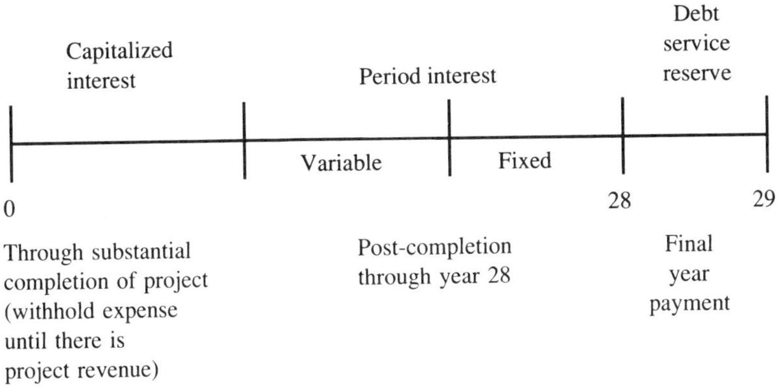

of the difficulty of predicting either the timing of a conversion of short-term debt or the interest rate on such debt while it is in either the short- or long-term mode. Unless these factors can be reasonably predicted, the use of estimated leveled interest rates would not be appropriate.

Capitalization of Interest

Interest on external debt should be capitalized as part of the historical cost of acquiring plant assets. Interest capitalization is required for those assets if its effect, compared with the effect of treating interest as a period expense, is material. If the effect is not material, interest capitalization is not required. The general objectives of capitalizing interest in a for-profit environment are (1) to obtain a measure of acquisition cost that more closely reflects the institution's total investment in the asset and (2) to charge cost which relates to the acquisition of a resource that will benefit future periods against the revenues of the periods benefited.

THEORY OF CAPITALIZATION

In the college and university environment, it makes sense to withhold debt service from the expense stream during the construction period, when the building is not in use, and spread the debt service expense (including amortization of issuance costs) to periods when it is generating revenue. (Because an educational institution charges current funds operations for debt service under the audit guide—not interest alone—it is conceivable that principal, as well as interest, could be capitalized. In practice, this is unlikely because most debt issues defer principal repayment during the construction period.)

INTEREST QUALIFYING FOR CAPITALIZATION

Colleges and universities frequently encounter situations in which assets qualifying for capitalization of interest are financed with the proceeds of restricted tax-exempt borrowings. In these cases, the amount of interest cost to be capitalized is all the debt service cost of those borrowings less any interest earned on temporary investment of the proceeds of those borrowings (including interest earned and paid on debt service reserves), from the date of borrowing until the specified assets acquired with those borrowings are ready for their intended use.

In other situations, the interest cost eligible for capitalization is the cost recognized on general borrowings and other obligations. The amount capitalized is an allocation of the interest cost incurred during the period required to complete the asset. Such capitalization of interest on general borrowing would not be allowed, however, on qualifying assets acquired using gifts or grants that were restricted by the donor to the project, as long as available gifts and grants exceed construction costs incurred. In all cases, the amount of interest cost to be capitalized is intended to be the portion of interest cost incurred during the assets' acquisition periods that theoretically could have been avoided (for example, by avoiding specific additional borrowings or by using funds expended for the assets to repay existing borrowings) if expenditures for the assets had not been made. Exhibit 25 illustrates capitalization choices.

THE PERIOD OF CAPITALIZATION

The amount of debt service capitalized is determined by applying a capitalization rate to the average accumulated expenditures for the assets, during the period beginning when (1) expenditures for the asset have been made, (2) activities that are necessary to get the asset ready for its intended use are in progress, and (3) interest cost is incurred, to the date when the asset is substantially complete and ready for its intended use.

THE CAPITALIZATION RATE

For assets funded by specific borrowings, the capitalization rate is

EXHIBIT 25
Capitalization of Interest

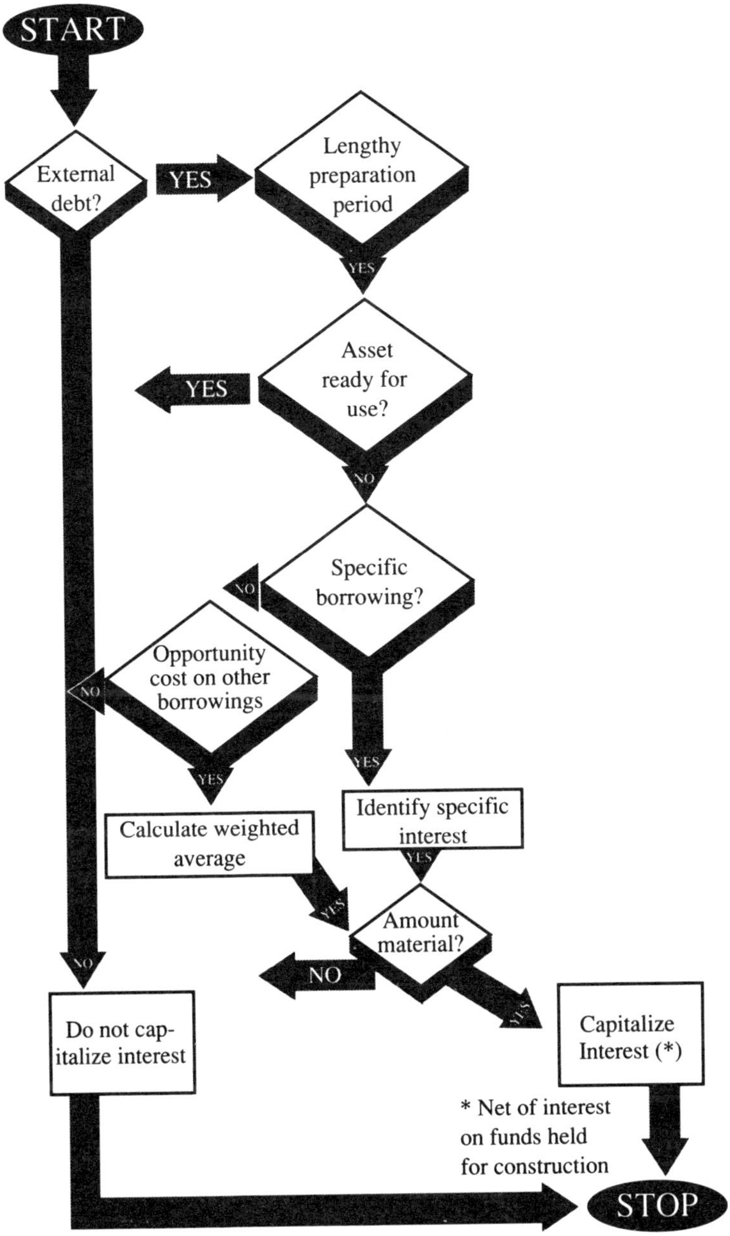

the interest rate for the period; for others, the aggregate average borrowing rate on general debts of the institution is used. Where all debt is associated with particular projects, interest on these borrowings is available for capitalization on other projects when the qualifying assets specified by that debt issue are no longer available for interest capitalization. There may be periods wherein the institution earns net interest either on the unexpended proceeds of debt or on unexpended gifts or grants. In such cases, the interest earnings would be capitalized as a deduction from the asset account: The institution's net cost of the asset would be less than its expenditures for bricks and mortar. Capitalized interest may be funded from the proceeds of certain bond issues. This source of funding should not affect the accounting treatment.

ALLOCATION OF CAPITALIZED INTEREST

In allocating interest costs among projects, most institutions use the proportion of project costs budgeted for each project, to the aggregate budgeted costs for all projects funded by the issue, then apply this ratio to total net interest cost during the construction period. Where more precise allocation is needed for purposes of departmental budgets or federal recovery, some institutions may calculate actual monthly balances for each project and allocate interest that way. In each period some projects may be charged interest and others may receive net credits for interest earned, while for a third category of completed projects no interest may be capitalized. Systems to allocate interest in such situations may be quite complex. Amounts of interest capitalized are eventually charged to fund balances through depreciation. There is no need to adjust amounts previously capitalized when an issue is refunded.

The example in appendix 9, from Statement of Financial Accounting Standards no. 62, illustrates the application of guidelines for capitalizing interest.

Extinguishment of Debt

An educational institution may consider debt to be extinguished for financial reporting purposes when:

- the institution repays the debt,
- the institution is legally released from its primary obligation to pay the debt, or

- the institution completes an "in-substance defeasance" of the debt.

Exhibit 26 illustrates the choices related to extinguishment.

EXTINGUISHING DEBT BY REPAYMENT

Repayment of debt is the most common method of extinguishment. Repayment also includes an institution's reacquisition of its debt in the open market, regardless of whether the debt securities are canceled or held as Treasury bonds. All repayments of debt are to be considered extinguishments if the institution is relieved of its obligations with respect to the debt.

EXTINGUISHING DEBT BY THIRD-PARTY ASSUMPTION

The second circumstance for extinguishment of debt occurs when an institution is legally released from being the primary obligor under the debt and when it is probable that the institution will not be required to make future payments with respect to that debt under any guarantees. *Probable* in this context is as defined in accounting standards for accounting for contingencies. This circumstance covers those transactions in which an institution's debt is assumed by a third party. For example, an institution may sell the net assets of a loan fund that has incurred long-term debt. To remove the debt of that fund from its books, the institution must be legally released from the role of primary obligor under the debt. Another requirement is the high probability that the institution will not be required to make any future payments on the debt.

Whether legal release from the role of primary obligor has been obtained will depend on the terms of the transaction, the terms of the debt agreement, and the provisions of various state laws. An opinion of legal counsel may be necessary to determine whether the legal release criterion has been met. In addition, where the original debtor remains secondarily liable, it must be probable that no future payments will be required under that secondary obligation before the debt can be removed from the debtor's balance sheet.

IN-SUBSTANCE DEFEASANCE

An in-substance defeasance of debt occurs when an institution

EXHIBIT 26
Extinguishment of Debt

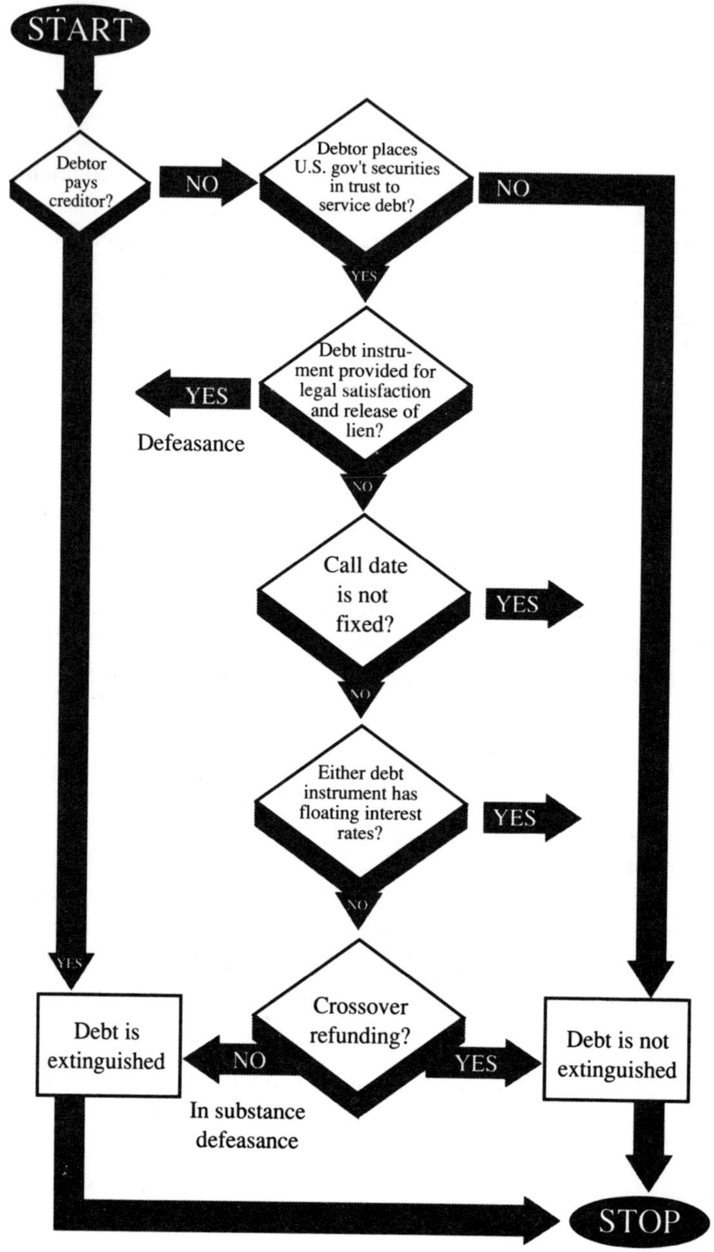

creates a trust and irrevocably funds it with appropriate monetary assets so that the cash flows from the trust assets will meet the interest and principal payments on the debt. For example, assume that an institution decides to defease $10 million of its 9 percent term bonds due in, or with a par call date in, ten years. The institution might create a trust and irrevocably fund it with $10 million par value, 9 percent U.S. Treasury bonds maturing in ten years, which were purchased at a discount for $8.3 million. The interest from the Treasury bonds would cover the interest payments on the debt, and, when the Treasury bonds matured, the maturity value of $10 million would be sufficient to repay the principal of the debt.

When extinguishment is deemed to have occurred, the debt is removed from the balance sheet and any resulting gain or loss is recognized. In the simple in-substance defeasance example above, a gain before taxes of $1.7 million would be recorded, since it cost the institution $8.3 million to purchase Treasury bonds that would repay debt carried on its books at $10 million. The gain would be reduced for the amount of unamortized issuance costs, which would be written off on the debt. If the debt funded plant assets, this gain would be recorded in the plant fund.

In-substance defeasance of debt is the only circumstance under which an institution may consider debt to be extinguished without a release from its position as primary obligor under the debt. Consequently, the Financial Accounting Standards Board (FASB) has set very strict requirements that an institution must meet in order to extinguish debt by in-substance defeasance. In summary, those requirements are that:

- the debt being defeased must have specified maturities and fixed payments schedules,
- the issuer must irrevocably place essentially risk-free assets in a trust to be used solely to satisfy the debt service requirement,
- the possibility that any further payments on the debt will be required by the institution must be remote.

The gain or loss on defeasance would be accounted for in the fund in which the debt resides. For completed projects, this would be net investment in plant. The remainder of this section discusses the specific requirements of the FASB regarding in-substance defeasance of debt.

IDENTIFYING DEBT THAT MAY BE EXTINGUISHED

Since the likelihood of the institution's being required to make additional payments with respect to the debt must be remote, the assets in the trust must be the sole source of cash flows to meet the debt interest and principal payments. Thus, for debt to qualify for extinguishment by in-substance defeasance, it must have fixed payment amounts and maturities. Any debt whose maturities and payment amounts are fixed may be defeased, including, for example, capitalized lease obligations.

Debt with a floating interest rate may not be defeased, since the amount of future interest payments is not known. Similarly, capitalized lease obligations that provide for contingent rentals may not be defeased. Debt with a "put" option by the holder may not be defeased.

NATURE AND DISPOSITION OF TRUST ASSETS

The trust must own only monetary assets that are essentially risk free with regard to the amount, timing, and collection of interest and principal. The FASB has indicated that it is not appropriate to apply a "remoteness" test when considering whether a security is essentially risk free. This strict requirement could prohibit the use of certain securities that might otherwise be attractive for funding a trust.

Risk-free monetary assets are limited to:

- direct obligations of the U.S. government,
- obligations guaranteed by the U.S. government, and
- securities that are backed by U.S. government obligations as collateral under an arrangement by which the interest and principal payments on the collateral generally flow immediately through to the holder of the security.

U.S. Treasury bonds, Treasury bills, and other direct obligations may be used to fund a trust. Obligations of U.S. government agencies would only qualify if they are guaranteed by the U.S. government. However, a security with a government guarantee that provides for the ultimate, but not the timely, collection of principal and interest (such as a GNMA security) would not qualify for ownership by the trust.

Certain investments in closed trusts marketed by investment bankers, which provide unit ownership interests in pools of U.S. Treasury obligations ("CATS" or "TIGRS") would qualify for funding the trust if they are directly collateralized by the principal or interest coupons of specific Treasury obligations and if the proceeds from the collection of principal and interest on the collateral securities pass immediately to the holder. However, investments collateralized by callable Treasury obligations would generally not qualify as trust assets since they are

EXHIBIT 27
Comparison of High to Low Advance Refunding Methods

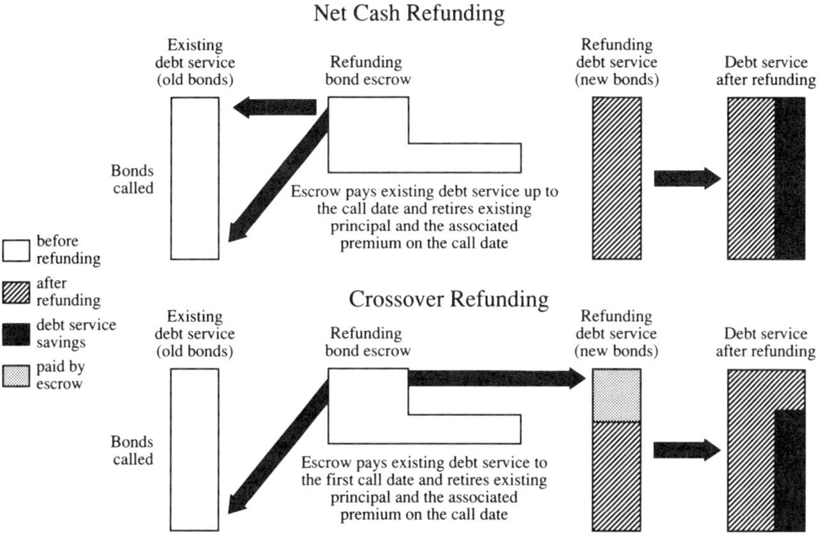

Source: Goldman Sachs.

not essentially risk free with regard to the timing of interest and principal payments.

The trust must be designed so that neither the institution nor others can rescind or revoke it or gain access to the assets. The trustee may change investments at a later date.

CALLABLE DEBT

Debt that may be called by the issuer may be extinguished through in-substance defeasance in certain circumstances. Since only debt that has specified maturities can be defeased, the institution should decide at the time of the extinguishment whether the debt will be paid at maturity or at an earlier call date. The institution must either resolve not to exercise the call provisions of the debt (and take the necessary action to renounce its ability to call the debt in the future) or resolve to call the debt at a specific date. The trust agreements should specify the date at which the trustee is to repay the debt. If the institution resolves to have the debt called at a specific date, the trust should be funded to meet the required debt service payments up to that call date, including any applicable call premium.

INSTANTANEOUS DEFEASANCE

Debt may not be issued and immediately extinguished by in-substance defeasance. Such a transaction is considered a simultaneous borrowing and investment, and the related income and expense would be recognized over the course of the issue. Similarly, crossover issues do not qualify for in-substance defeasance because the old debt is not extinguished. Exhibit 27 compares net advance refunding with crossover extinguishment.

Chapter 8
Federal Recovery

Costs incurred for external interest on borrowed capital are allowable under Office of Management and Budget Circular A-21, where associated with building renovation or acquisition of capital equipment (the latter with sponsor's approval) after July 1982, provided that the assets are used in support of sponsored agreements and the total cost does not exceed comparable rentals in the same locality.

Interest capitalization and debt defeasance , as discussed previously, would apply, since federal cost regulations are designed to be substantially consistent with generally accepted accounting principles. Net capitalized interest would be recovered for eligible projects through depreciation or use allowance. The periods over which depreciation and interest are recovered might be different; if so, for simplicity of calculation, those periods should be followed. Internal interest on current or endowment fund borrowings would not be allowed. Periodic net interest cost is most appropriately recovered through the operations and maintenance cost pool. Interest costs related to major specialized service centers would be recovered through their separate rates. Treatment of gains or losses on debt defeasance would most likely be taken over time, and specifically resolved on a case-by-case basis.

In general, the recovery pattern would follow as illustrated in exhibit 28. The university would recover interest and depreciation and pay level debt service. At the start, the recovery would exceed the payments (note the area between the depreciation curve and the straight line for level debt service on the left), while interest would drop off at the end, when debt service would exceed the amount of recovery. In many cases, the university may be able to accumulate a replacement fund from the additional recoveries at the start of the project.

It should be clear that the principal outstanding on level payment or mortgage debt decreases more slowly than the net asset value (see exhibit 29).

In fact, there may be no correlation between the asset life and the maturity. Therefore, the principal outstanding at any given time is more than the net asset after depreciation (see exhibit 30).

EXHIBIT 28
Level Debt Service

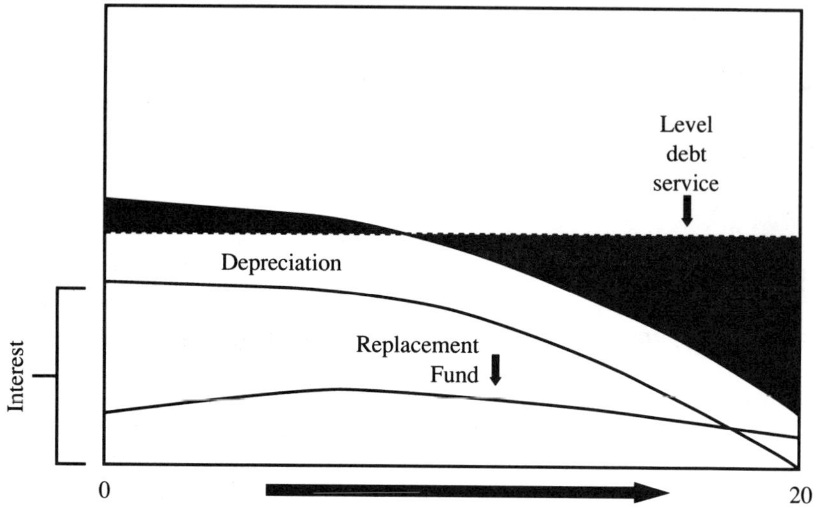

EXHIBIT 29
Principal Outstanding
30-year debt, 30-year asset

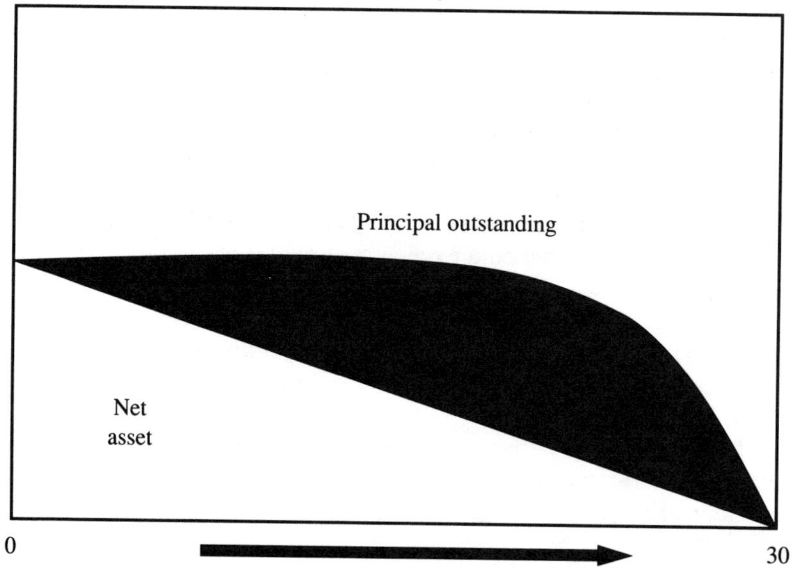

EXHIBIT 30
Principal Outstanding
30-year debt, 20-year asset

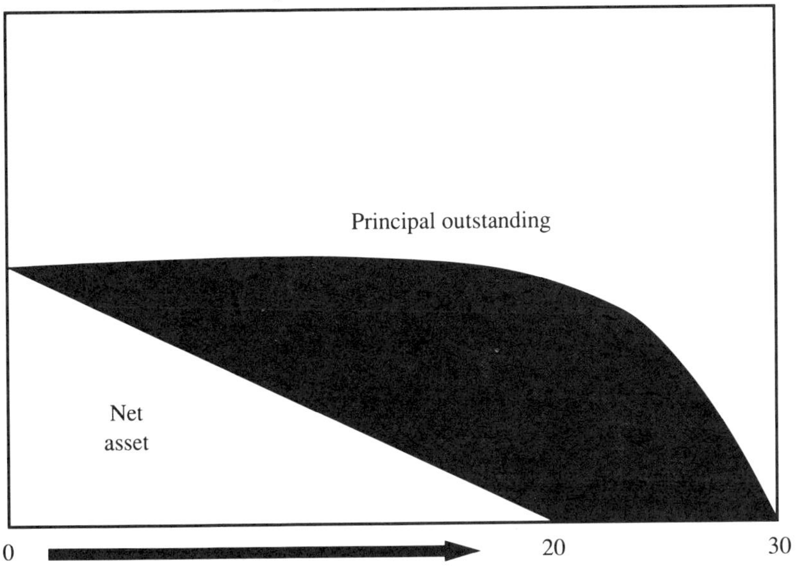

If an institution was to invest depreciation recoveries that were in excess of principal amounts paid, this accumulated amount, as described above, could serve as support for institutional creditworthiness.

In this case, a $10 million building is depreciated over 20 years, while the related debt is paid on a mortgage or level payment basis over 30 years. The source of cash (depreciation recovery) in excess of the use of the cash (payment of principal) is invested in a recovery fund. At the end of the net asset life, 20 years, $16.8 million is available in this fund. (This amount is analogous to the $1.45 million in the NYNEX depreciation fund described in the first chapter.) At the end of 30 years, however, this recovery fund has grown to $50 million—five times the original asset (see exhibit 31). The previous chapter, however, described a trend away from associating a particular debt issue, and its related debt service, with a single asset. It looked forward to the time when universities would aspire to an ideal capital structure—one that included optimum amounts of debt and equity. Debt associated with a particular asset, then, might conceivably not be repaid.

EXHIBIT 31
Federal Recovery

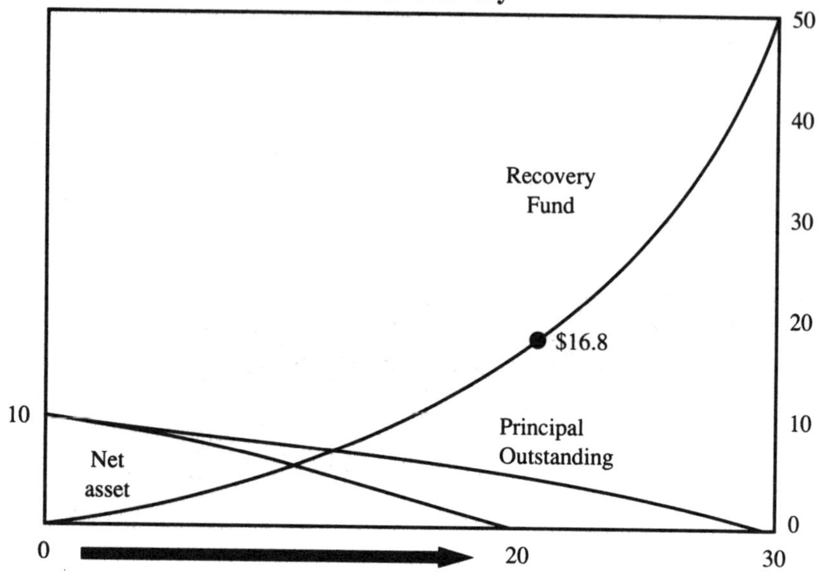

EXHIBIT 32
Cost of Money

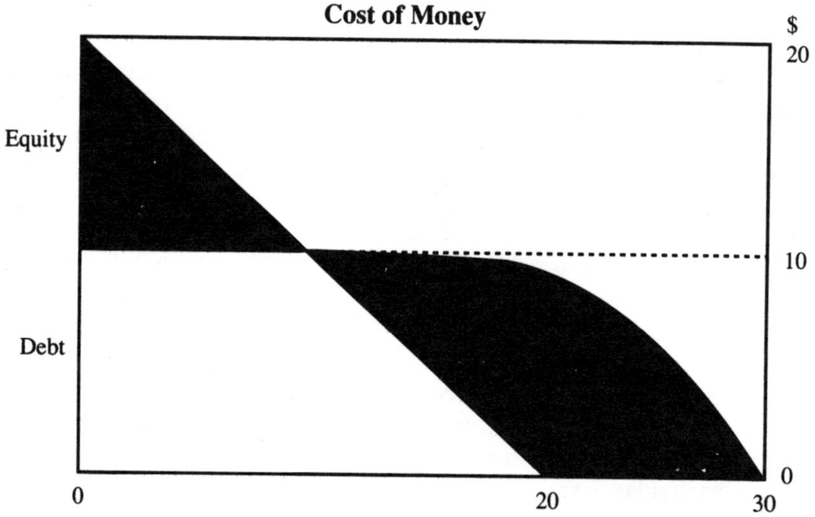

In the commercial sector, recovery is accomplished somewhat differently. Instead, under Cost Accounting Standard 414, contractors recover the cost of money, for both debt and equity investments, at the 91-day Treasury bill rate, over the depreciation period for the asset. Exhibit 32 illustrates this recovery in comparison with recovery of interest on level payment debt. One can see that recoveries are higher at the start, but this effect is offset later on, since the depreciation period is shorter than the life of the debt.

In time, the government may choose this method of reimbursement for colleges and universities as well.

Appendix 1
Examples of Debt Accounting

Example A: Bank Financing

XYZ University plans to borrow $1,200,000 to build a new dormitory. The note is payable in three equal annual installments and bears interest at an annual rate of 8 percent. XYZ can call the note at the end of the first year. XYZ plans to fund the debt service from current funds. The proceeds are received in advance and construction of the dormitory takes one year to complete.

Other Assumptions

1. Debt issued at face amount, i.e., no premium or discount.
2. No bond issuance costs associated with the issuance of debt.
3. Interest capitalized in accordance with Statement of Financial Accounting Standards (SFAS) no. 34, "Interest Capitalization."
4. Note is called and debt refunded at the end of year 1.
5. No other projects of the university are currently under construction.

Example A—Bank Financing

Event/Explanation	Current Unrestricted Fund			Unexpended Plant Fund		
YEAR 1						
I. Original issuance						
• XYZ borrows $1,200,000. Construction of new dormitory				Cash	$1,200,000	
				Note payable		$1,200,000
• Cash is expended for construction costs evenly throughout year 1				Construction work in progress (CWIP)	1,200,000	
				Cash		1,200,000
• To capitalize CWIP expended to net investment-in-plant fund				Note payable	1,200,000	
				CWIP		1,200,000
II. Debt service						
• Year 1 interest expense funded	Mandatory transfer	$ 96,000				
	Cash		$96,000			
• Year 1 interest expense payment						
• Year 1 principal payment funded	Mandatory transfer	400,000				
	Cash		400,000			
• Year 1 principal payment						
III. Interest capitalization (SFAS no. 34)						
• Average accumulated expenditures for construction period ($1,200,000 ÷ 2 = $600,000) × interest rate (8%)						
IV. Refunding						
• Interest rates drop to 6%. XYZ renegotiates remaining principal balance of $800,000 for a new rate at 6.5% and balance of $810,000						

Retirement-of-Indebtedness Fund			Net Investment-in-Plant Fund		
			Property and plant	$1,200,000	
			Note payable		$1,200,000
Cash	$ 96,000				
Mandatory transfer		$96,000			
Interest expense	96,000				
Cash		96,000			
Cash	400,000				
Mandatory transfer		400,000			
Decrease in fund balance	400,000		Note payable	400,000	
Cash		400,000	Increase in fund balance		400,000
			Property and plant	48,000	
			Increase in fund balance		48,000
			Loss on refunding	10,000	
			Note payable		10,000

Event/Explanation	Current Unrestricted Fund			Unexpended Plant Fund
YEAR 2				
I. Original issuance No entry required.				
II. Debt service				
• Year 2 interest expense funded ($810,000 × 6.5%)	Mandatory transfer Cash	$ 52,650	 $52,650	
• Year 2 interest expense payment				
• Year 2 principal payment funded	Mandatory transfer Cash	405,000	 405,000	
• Year 2 principal payment				
III. Interest capitalization No interest cost capitalized as total expenditues were incurred during Year 1. No other specific projects of the university currently under construction.				
IV. Refunding No entry required.				
YEAR 3				
I. Original issuance No entry required				
II. Debt service				
• Year 3 interest expense funded ($405,000 × 6.5%)	Mandatory transfer Cash	26,325	 26,325	
• Year 3 interest expense payment				
• Year 3 principal payment funded	Mandatory transfer Cash	405,000	 405,000	
• Year 3 principal payment				
III. Interest capitalization No interest cost capitalized as total expenditures were incurred during year 1. No other specific projects of the university currently under construction.				
IV. Refunding No entry required.				

Retirement-of-Indebtedness Fund			Net Investment-in-Plant Fund		
Cash	$ 52,650				
Mandatory transfer		$ 52,650			
Interest expense	52,650				
Cash		52,650			
Cash	405,000				
Mandatory transfer		405,000			
Decrease in fund balance	405,000		Note payable	$ 405,000	
Cash		405,000	Increase in fund balance		405,000
Cash	26,325				
Mandatory transfer		26,325			
Interest expense	26,325				
Cash		26,325			
Cash	405,000				
Mandatory transfer		405,000			
Decrease in fund balance	405,000		Note payable	405,000	
Cash		405,000	Increase in fund balance		405,000

Example B: Tax-Exempt Financing

XYZ University plans to issue $1,200,000 in revenue bonds through the State Health and Educational Facilities Authority to build a new dormitory and library. The revenue bonds are payable in three equal annual installments and bear interest at an annual rate of 5 percent. The construction of the dormitory and library will take two years to complete. XYZ plans to fund the debt service from current funds. Construction and debt service reserve funds on deposit with the trustee are invested in United States Treasury bills. The average T-bill rate was 6 percent for years 1 through 3. The proceeds received from the sale of the bonds will be applied as follows:

Estimated cost of dormitory	$ 600,000
Estimated cost of library	300,000
Costs of issuance	150,000
Discount on sale of bonds	50,000
For deposit in the debt service reserve fund	100,000
Principal amount of bonds	$1,200,000

Other Assumptions

1. Amortization of bond discount and issuance costs is based upon straight-line amortization, which approximates interest method.
2. Construction work in progress and related debt are transferred to net investment in plant fund as funds are expended.
3. Debt service payments decrease bonds payable in net investment-in-plant fund prior to reducing debt associated with bond issuance costs and bond discount to the extent construction funds expended exceed debt service payments.
4. Actual project costs equal estimated project costs.
5. Projects are completed at the end of year 2 and ready for intended use.
6. Interest income earned on construction funds on deposit will be used to pay principal on bonds in year 3.
7. Year 3 principal payment made to the authority at the end of the year.

Example B—Tax Exempt Financing

Event/Explanation	Current Unrestricted Fund			Unexpended Plant Fund		
YEAR 1						
I. Original issuance (including recognition of bond issuance costs and discount on sale of bonds)						
• XYZ University borrows $1,200,000 to finance construction of a new dormitory and library and the application of proceeds is recorded				Deposit with trustee	$900,000	
				Bonds payable		$900,000
• Cash is drawn down and expended for construction during year 1						
• $300,000—dormitory $200,000—library				Cash	500,000	
				Deposit with trustee		500,000
				Construction work in Progress	500,000	
				Cash		500,000
• To capitalize CWIP expended in net investment-in-plant fund				Bonds payable	500,000	
				CWIP		500,000
II. Bond discount and issuance costs						
• To amortize bond issuance costs and discount on sale of bonds in Year 1						
• Amortization of bond discount $50,000 ÷ 3 years = $16,667						
• Amortization of bond issuance costs $150,000 ÷ 3 years = $50,000						
III. Debt service						
• Year 1 interest expense (5% × $1,200,00) funded	Mandatory transfer	$ 60,000				
	Cash		$ 60,000			
• Year 1 interest expense payment						
• Year 1 principal payment funded	Mandatory transfer	400,000				
	Cash		400,000			
• Year 1 principal payment made						

Retirement-of-Indebtedness Fund			Net Investment-in-Plant Fund		
Deposit with trustee	$100,000				
Discount on sale of bonds	50,000				
Bond issuance costs	150,000				
Bonds payable		$300,000			
			Dormitory	$300,000	
			Library	200,000	
			Bonds payable		$500,000
Interest expense	16,667				
Amortization of bond issuance costs	50,000				
Discount on sale of bonds		16,667			
Bond issuance costs		50,000			
Cash	60,000				
Mandatory transfer		60,000			
Interest expense	60,000				
Cash		60,000			
Cash	400,000				
Mandatory transfer		400,000			
Decrease in fund balance	400,000		Bonds payable	400,000	
Cash		400,000	Increase in fund balance		400,000

Event/Explanation	Current Unrestricted Fund			Unexpended Plant Fund		
IV. Interest Capitalization						
• To record interest income earned on debt service reserve fund ($100,000 on deposit × 6%)	Due from retirement of indebtedness fund	$ 6,000				
	Interest income		$ 6,000			
• To record capitalization of interest expense (see question/interpretation no. 2)						
• To record capitalization of interest income (see question/interpretation no. 2—as income may be used to retire debt it may be appropriate to record in retirement-of-indebtedness fund)				Deposit with trustee	$ 39,000	
				Interest income		$ 39,000
YEAR 2						
I. Construction drawdowns						
• Cash is drawndown for construction in year 2						
• $300,000—dormitory $100,000—library				Cash	400,000	
				Deposit with trustee		400,000
				CWIP	400,000	
				Cash		400,000
• To capitalize CWIP expended in net investment-in-plant fund				Bonds payable	400,000	
				CWIP		400,000
II. Bond discount and issuance costs						
• To amortize bond issuance costs and discounts on sale of bonds in year 2						

Retirement-of-Indebtedness Fund			Net Investment-in-Plant Fund		
Deposit with trustee	$ 6,000				
Due to current unrestricted fund		$ 6,000			
			Library	$ 21,359	
			Dormitory	42,778	
			Increase in fund balance		$ 64,167
			Decrease in fund balance	39,000	
			Library		12,000
			Dormitory		27,000
			Dormitory	300,000	
			Library	100,000	
			Bonds payable		400,000
Interest expense	16,667				
Amortization of bond issuance costs	50,000				
Discount on sale of bonds		16,667			
Bond issuance costs		50,000			

Event/Explanation	Current Unrestricted Fund			Unexpended Plant Fund		
III. Debt service						
• Year 2 interest expense funded	Mandatory transfer Cash	$ 60,000	 $ 60,000			
• Year 2 interest expense payment						
• Year 2 principal payment funded	Mandatory transfer Cash	400,000	 400,000			
• Year 2 principal payment made						
IV. Interest capitalization						
• To record interest income earned on debt service reserve fund ($100,000 on deposit × 6%)	Due from retirement of indebtendess fund Interest income	6,000	 6,000			
• To record capitalization of interest expense (see question/interpretation no. 2)						
• To record capitalization of interest income (see question/interpretation no. 2)				Deposit with trustee Interest income	$ 12,000	 $ 12,000
YEAR 3						
I. Construction drawdowns						
• No activity—projects completed						
II. Bond discount and issuance costs						
• To amortize bond issuance costs and discount on sale of bonds in Year 3						
III. Debt service						
• Year 3 interest expense funded	Mandatory transfer Cash	60,000	 60,000			
• Year 3 interest expense payment						
• Year 3 principal payment funded	Mandatory transfer Cash Due from retirement of indebtedness fund	249,000 18,000	 231,000			

Retirement-of-Indebtedness Fund			Net Investment-in-Plant Fund		
Cash	$ 60,000				
Mandatory transfer		$ 60,000			
Interest expense	60,000				
Cash		60,000			
Cash	400,000				
Mandatory transfer		400,000			
Decrease in fund balance	$400,000		Bonds payable	$400,000	
Cash		$400,000	Increase in fund balance		$400,000
Deposit with trustee	6,000				
Due to current unrestricted fund		6,000			
			Library	21,389	
			Dormitory	42,778	
			Increase in fund balance		64,167
			Decrease in fund balance	12,000	
			Library		9,000
			Dormitory		3,000
Interest expense	16,667				
Amortization of bond issuance costs	50,000				
Discount on sale of bonds		16,667			
Bond issuance costs		50,000			
Cash	60,000				
Mandatory transfer		60,000			
Interest expense	60,000				
Cash		60,000			
Cash	231,000				
Due to current unrestricted	18,000				
Mandatory transfer		249,000			

Event/Explanation	Current Unrestricted Fund			Unexpended Plant Fund		
• To drawdown interest earned on construction funds				Cash	$ 51,000	
				Deposit with trustee		$ 51,000
• To transfer interest earned on construction fund to retirement-of-indebtedness fund for payment of debt				Other transfer	51,000	
				Cash		51,000
• To drawdown debt service reserve fund and accumulated income						
• Year 3 principal payment made						
IV. Interest capitalization						
• To record interest income earned on debt service reserve fund ($100,000 on deposit × 6%)	Due from retirement of indebtedness fund	$ 6,000				
	Interest income		$ 6,000			
• No interest capitalization—projects completed in year 2 and ready for their intended use at that time						

Retirement-of-Indebtedness Fund			Net Investment-in-Plant Fund		
Cash	$ 51,000				
Other transfer		$ 51,000			
Cash	118,000				
Deposit with trustee		118,000			
Bonds payable	100,000				
Cash		100,000			
Bonds payable	200,000		Bonds payable	$100,000	
Decrease in fund balance	100,000		Increase in fund balance		$100,000
Cash		300,000			
Deposit with trustee	$ 6,000				
Due to current unrestricted fund		$ 6,000			

Appendix 2

Questions/Interpretations Regarding Debt Accounting

1. Question

How is the capitalization of interest cost under SFAS 62 handled when a specific project is over or under budget?

Interpretations

When a project is over budget, i.e., the proceeds of the debt are not sufficient to complete the qualified asset and make it ready for its intended use, the capitalization of interest cost could be continued to the extent that interest is being paid on other external debt in accordance with SFAS no. 62.

When a project is recognized to be under budget, i.e., the proceeds exceed the amount needed to complete the qualified assets, one interpretation would be that interest capitalization would depend on the institution's intent to apply for additional projects or refunding. If it is the intent to apply for usage of the funds for other projects, interest cost may continue to be capitalized on the overfunded debt even though no project has yet to be specifically identified. If it is likely that the amounts will be refunded, interest capitalization should cease.

2. Question

When a tax-exempt issue is earmarked for more than one project, on what basis should interest income and cost be capitalized?

Interpretations

One interpretation would capitalize interest income and cost on the basis of construction fund balances and the portion of debt earmarked for construction only. The interest cost and interest earned on any portion of the proceeds of a tax-exempt borrowing that are not designated for the construction of specific qualifying assets and servicing the related debt would be excluded from capitalization. Assets held for debt service reserve provisions and the related debt would not be considered in the allocation. Assume $1,200,000, 5 percent revenue bonds issued, $900,000 earmarked for construction, and $100,000 for a debt service reserve fund. The funds are earmarked for two projects with budgets of $600,000 and $300,000, respectively. Interest cost could be allocated as follows:

	Budget	Percent of Total	Annual Interest Cost (5% rate)
Project 1—dormitory	$ 600,000	66.67	$30,000
Project 2—library	300,000	33.33	15,000
		100.00	
Total budgeted costs for projects	900,000		45,000
Discount on sale of bonds	50,000		2,500
	950,000		47,500
Bond issuance costs	150,000		7,500
Debt service reserve fund	100,000		5,000
Total issue	$1,200,000		$60,000

	Project 1 dormitory 66.67%	Project 2 library 33.33%	Total
Annual interest cost (based upon project budgets)	$31,667	$15,833	$47,500
Annual amortization of discount—discount on sale of bonds	11,111	5,556	16,667
	$42,778	$21,389	$64,167

Another interpretation would include interest expense and interest income earned on the debt service reserve fund in considering the net interest cost to be capitalized.

Allocation of interest income:

One interpretation would be to allocate interest income on the basis of average construction fund balances determined on a periodic basis (e.g., monthly) to best estimate the amount of income earned on assets held for specific projects:

Year 1

	Budget	Draw Downs	Balance	Average	Percent	Annual Interest Income (6% rate)
Project 1	$600,000	$(300,000)	$300,000	$ 50,000	69.23	$27,000
Project 2	300,000	(200,000)	100,000	200,000	30.77	12,000
	$900,000	$(500,000)	$400,000	$650,000	100.00	$39,000

Year 2

	Budget	Draw Downs	Balance	Average	Percent	Annual Interest Income (6% rate)
Project 1	$300,000	$(300,000)	-0-	$150,000	75.00	$ 9,000
Project 2	100,000	(100,000)	-0-	50,000	25.00	3,000
	$400,000	$(400,000)	-0-	$200,000	100.00	$12,000

A second interpretation would be to allocate interest income earned on unspent construction funds equally to individual projects without regard to the project fund balances generating the earnings.

3. Question

If debt is called and reissued at a different rate, should interest previously capitalized be adjusted?

Interpretations

One interpretation would not adjust interest cost previously capitalized on the theory that interest should be capitalized at the rates in effect during the construction period and is reflective of the interest cost that would have been avoided if other funds were used. Another interpretation would adjust previous interest cost capitalized to reflect a net borrowing cost considering the refunding.

4. Question

In which plant fund subgroup should debt and assets related to the debt service reserve fund be maintained (e.g., unexpended plant fund or fund for retirement of indebtedness)?

Interpretations

Funds on deposit with a trustee to satisfy a debt service reserve fund requirement should be maintained in the fund for retirement of indebtedness in accordance with the AICPA Audit Guide for Colleges and Universities.

5. Question

In which fund should interest income earned on debt service reserve fund assets be recognized during the term of the bond?

Interpretations

One interpretation would recognize interest income earned on the debt service reserve fund in the current fund during the term of the bond on the theory that this income would reduce the final year debt service transfer from current funds and is not designated for the acquisition of specified qualifying assets.

Another interpretation would consider debt service fund income in the capitalization of net interest cost (i.e., designated for the acquisition of specified qualifying assets). In this case, income would be recognized in the retirement of indebtedness fund.

6. Question

Should interest income earned on unexpended construction fund balance be capitalized for projects not yet begun?

Interpretations

In accordance with SFAS no. 62, interest income earned on related interest-bearing investments acquired with the proceeds of related tax-exempt borrowings should be capitalized from the date of the borrowing until the assets are ready for their intended use.

7. Question

At what interest rate should interest cost be capitalized?

Interpretations

In accordance with SFAS no. 34, the amount capitalized in an accounting period shall be determined by applying an interest rate (the capitalization rate) to the average amount of accumulated expenditures for the asset during the period. The capitalization rates used in an accounting period shall be based on the rates applicable to borrowings outstanding during the period. If an institution's financing plans associate a specific new borrowing with a qualifying asset, the institution may use the rate on that borrowing as the capitalization rate to be applied to that portion of the average accumulated expenditures for the asset that does not exceed the amount of that borrowing. If average accumulated expenditures for the asset exceed the amounts of specific new borrowings associated with the asset, the capitalization rate to be applied to such excess shall be a weighted average rate applicable to other borrowings of the institution.

For tax-exempt financing, SFAS no. 62 states that the interest cost capitalized shall be the interest cost of the borrowing less any interest earned on related interest-bearing investments acquired with the proceeds of the related tax-exempt borrowings.

8. Question

How should bond issuance costs on refunded debt be treated?

Interpretations

In most cases, bond issuance costs on refunded debt should be written off at the time of refunding.

9. Question

At what rate should bond premium or discount be recognized? Should premium or discount be capitalized?

Interpretations

Bond premium or discount on bonds should be recognized as an adjustment of interest expense over the period of maturity of the debt generally in proportion to the recognition of interest expense. The interest method of amortization should be used. The straight-line method could be used, however, if its results do not materially differ from those of the interest method. If interest expense is capitalized during a period of construction, amortized discount or premium should also be capitalized during the same period.

10. Question

Is interest expense of a tax-exempt borrowing eligible for capitalization on other qualifying assets of the institution when the specified assets have been completed?

Interpretations

In accordance with SFAS no. 62, interest cost of a tax-exempt borrowing shall be eligible for other qualifying assets of the institution when the specified qualifying assets are no longer eligible for interest capitalization.

11. Question

In which fund should a gain or loss on refunding of debt be recognized?

Interpretations

Most institutions would record a gain or loss on refunding of debt in the fund in which the debt resides, i.e., unexpended plant fund for unexpended proceeds, and net investment-in-plant fund for proceeds expended. Other institutions would record the gain or loss in the current unrestricted fund, because this fund would be the ultimate debt funding source.

Appendix 3
Subject Bibliography

Advantages/Uses of Debt Financing

Baum, Rudy M. "Debt Financing: Academia's Funding Alternative." *Chemical & Engineering News* (June 1, 1981).

Describes various tax-exempt forms, gives several advantages to colleges and universities of using debt financing, and makes recommendations of what to consider before becoming involved with debt.

"Creative Financing for Higher Education Facilities and Equipment." Collected Works. *ERIC Reports* (1985).

The first article looks at the historical development of debt use; the second discusses the importance of debt management; the third points out the opportunities that the tax law offers; the fourth studies how debt financing can remedy the severe shortage of research project funds; and the final article recommends setting up a state-equipment fund to issue debt to build new equipment.

"Financial Planning for Energy Efficiency Investments." *Business Officer* (March 1984).

A summary of financing options is listed in table form followed by a discussion on how to choose among them. Project size, debt capacity, level of in-house expertise, and public/private status are suggested as decision criteria. In addition, financial analysis techniques for evaluating energy efficiency projects are discussed.

Henze, William F. II. "Designing Successful Multi-University Tax-Exempt Bond Issues." *Business Officer* (April 1983).

States that multiuniversity tax-exempt bonds are advantageous because tax-exempt financing gives lower interest costs and multiuniversity financing allows the up-front issuance costs to be spread out. Suggestions are given about how to organize the issues so as to attract large universities.

"Ivy League Bonds." *The Economist* (July 24, 1982).

Describes the use of tax-exempt bonds to make student loans through state agencies authorized to issue tax-free bonds and warns that the federal government may attempt to limit or stop such transactions.

Kaiser, Ronald B. "Debt Financing for the Support of University Research Programs." *SRA Journal* (spring 1981).

Discusses topics such as debt management, the use of nonprofit foundations, and the types of tax-exempt debt financing.

Mullner, Ross, Dale Matthews, Joseph D. Kubal, and Steven Andes. "Debt Financing: An Alternative for Hospital Construction Funding." *Healthcare Financial Management* (April 1983).

Shows trends of the use of debt financing in the health care industry by showing actual results of a study on funding sources of capital projects throughout the 1970s and early 1980s.

Debt Capacity

Beauford-Marcano, Rafael Emilio. "A Description, Analysis and Evaluation of the Financial Structure of Four Private Universities in the Consortium of Universites of the Washington Metropolitan Area between 1973–74 and 1982–83." Ph.D. diss., George Washington University, December 1984.

Gives an analysis of the financial structure of four universities by first describing the criteria to evaluate credit worthiness and then calculating and evaluating the characteristic.

Deets, M. King, and Susanna E. Krentz. "Hospital Debt Capacity in a Competitive Environment." *Healthcare Financial Management* (July 1982).

Attempts to predict the effects that deregulation, and thus competition, will have on the health care industry relating to bond ratings and debt capacity, through comparisons with both the public utility and airline industries.

Fitz, Thomas E., Jr. "Debt Capacity Analysis Is Critical to Planning." *Healthcare Financial Management* (January 1983).

Outlines the basic components of a debt capacity analysis, such as ratios and impact analysis, and gives an example related to a health care organization.

Mintner, John W. "The Financial Assessment of Colleges and Universities and Its Implication for State Policy." *ERIC Reports* (February 1978).

Describes the important issues and technical problems of assessing the financial health of colleges and universities, and discusses the likely implications for state boards of education.

Capitalization of Interest

"Capitalization of Interest Cost." *CPA Journal* (March 1981).

Discusses SFAS 34—Capitalization of Interest Costs as amended by SFAS 42—Determining Materiality . . ., and describes qualifying assets, the calculation of interest to be capitalized, limitations, and the necessary disclosures.

McTague, Edward. "Capitalizing Interest Cost: How to Make the Computations." *Practical Accountant* (November 1985).

Gives a walk-through example of making interest capitalization calculations under a hypothetical case in which quarterly accounting periods, more than one specific borrowing, more than one nonspecific borrowing, and differing interest rates are assumed.

Defeasances

"Extinguishment of Debt—SFAS 76." *CPA Journal* (April, 1984).

Offers a synopsis of SFAS 76, which primarily deals with defining those situations into which the defeasance of debt is considered to have occurred "in-substance."

Fazio, John A. " 'In-Substance Defeasance' Accounting Revised." *CPA Journal* (May 1984).

Agrees with SFAS 76 treatment of "in-substance defeasances" despite claims of critics that it allows "instant profits."

Gray, Dahli, and Mary Alice Seville. "In-Substance Defeasance:

Altering the Shape of Debt Management." *Journal of Accounting* (January 1985).

Describes the importance of in-substance defeasances by showing their effect on the financial statements and ratios when treated as extinguishments. Also describes in-substance defeasance with a flowchart and narrative.

Izard, Douglas, and Jan R. Williams. "How to Handle the Conflicting Accounting and Tax Rules That Come into Play When a Debt Is Extinguished." *The Practical Accountant* (April, 1986).

Discusses financial accounting treatment regarding the extinguishment of debt, the tax accounting treatment, and the differences between the two (particularly with respect to the recognition of a gain or loss). Summarizes differences in a table.

"SFAS No. 76—Extinguishment of Debt." *CPA Journal* (June 1984).

Flowchart depicts SFAS 76 accounting treatment for the debtor.

Debt's Relation to Overall Financial Management

Association of American Universities. *Financing and Managing University Research Equipment*. Washington, D.C.: AAU, 1985.

Gives a brief explanation of why debt financing for research equipment is usually state controlled. Discusses the various debt instruments, illustrates implementation, and outlines the advantages and disadvantages of each in table form.

Kaiser, Harvey H. "How Can We Afford This: Funding and Financing Means." *ERIC Reports* (February 1984).

Discusses the various sources of capital funding for colleges and universities, including debt financing and innovative techniques.

National Association of College and University Business Officers. *Financial Responsibilities of Governing Boards*. Washington, D.C.: NACUBO, 1985.

Gives general guidance on generating, spending, and managing the resources of colleges and universities, including the planning and budgeting process.

———. *A Planning Manual for Colleges.* Washington, D.C.: NACUBO, 1980.

Gives general guidance to the planning process, including the establishment of debt policy.

Phalon, Richard. "University As Venture Capitalist." *Forbes* (December 19, 1983).

Describes how Rennselaer Polytechnic Institute is trying to develop high-tech industry around Troy, N.Y., by using an "incubator program" to help high-tech start-up companies in the area.

Racki, Joan, and Joanne Reece. "Financing Higher Education Facility Needs in Idaho." *ERIC Reports* (April 1985).

Discusses a study to identify possible ways for the State Board of Education of Idaho to meet the growing requests for funds to improve educational facilities.

When Debt Financing Goes Bad

Bratton, Donald L., "Facilities Financing and the Department of Education." *ERIC Reports* (November 1982).

Gives advice from a college administrator on what to do when faced with loans in default, as well as what can be done to avoid problems before the situation becomes critical.

Dickmeyer, Nathan. *Financial Conditions of Colleges and Universities.* Washington, D.C.: NACUBO, 1983.

Attempts to assist the U.S. Department of Education in responding to the question of what to do about financially failing institutions.

Woodruff, A.E. "1980–1985: The Threats to Higher Education: Special Reference to Connecticut." *ERIC Reports* (May 1979).

Looks at the financial problems of Connecticut schools caused by overexpansion and some of the solutions related to debt.

Accounting Issues Related to Debt

American Institute of Certified Public Accountants. *Industry Audit Guide: Audits of Colleges and Universities.* AICPA, 1983.

Gives general guidance to fund accounting in colleges and universities.

———. *Statement of Position 85-1*. AICPA: January, 1985.

Considers the question of how funds restricted by debt instruments should be classified by health care organizations.

National Association of College and University Business Officers. *College and Universities Business Administration: Administrative Service*. Washington, D.C.: NACUBO, 1982.

Part V gives general guidance to fund accounting by colleges and universities.

Office of Management and Budget. *Circular A-21*. Washington, D.C.: OMB: February 26, 1979.

Government document outlines the rules concerning cost recovery by colleges and universities under grants, contracts, and other agreements with the federal government.

Peat Marwick. *Principles and Presentation: Higher Education* New York: Peat, Marwick, 1985.

Gives sample disclosures by various colleges and universities, as well as the results of a survey of accounting practices.

Scheps and Davidson. *Accounting for Colleges and Universities* (1970).

Textbook gives example entries to record the acquisition of plant funds from a bond issue through the retirement of the bonds.

Miscellaneous

Kaynar, Robert K. "Using Spreadsheet Modeling Techniques for Capital Project Review." *ERIC Reports* (May 1985).

Shows how computer spreadsheets can calculate the short- and long-term effects of various funding vehicles on university cash flow.

Appendix 4
Criteria by Various Credit-Rating Agencies

(5/31/86 data used unless otherwise stated)

	"A"-Rated Issues	"AA"-Rated Issues
Standard & Poor's		
Student enrollment (total FTE student body)	Stable	Stable to increasing
Admissions rate (applications vs. accepts)	50% to 70% (lower is better)	25% to 50%
Matriculation rate (accepts vs. registrants)	20% to 30% (higher is better)	30% to 50%
SAT Scores	1,000 to 1,200 (higher is better)	1,200 to 1,300
Student draw (national—beyond 200 mi. radius)	Primarily regional	National
Student/faculty ratio (FTE student body/ FTE faculty)	16:1 (lower is better)	13–10:1
Faculty competition	Regional	National
Education programs	Primarily undergraduate, some diversification	Undergraduate and graduate, diverse
Tuition as a percent of revenues (Tuition [incl. related fees]/educational & general revenues [excl. auxiliary & athletics])	50% to 60% (lower is better)	50% and lower

	"A"-Rated Issues	"AA"-Rated Issues
Endowment funds as a percent of unrestricted current fund expenses (total endowment [incl. quasi]/unrestricted current fund expenses [incl. auxiliary & athletics])	100% (higher is better)	200%
Endowment per FTE student (total endowment [incl. quasi-]/FTE student body)	$15,000 to $50,000 (higher is better)	$50,000 to $100,000
Financial operations	Good	Strong
Unrestricted current fund: fund balance as a percent of fund expenses (total current fund balance forward/unrestricted current fund expenses [incl. auxiliary & athletics])	5.0% (higher is better)	15.4%
Debt service as a percent of unrestricted current fund expenses (principal & interest/unrestricted current fund expenses [incl. auxiliary & athletics])	7.5% (lower is better)	5.20%
Debt as a percent of endowment (total outstanding long-term debt/total endowment [incl. quasi-])	75.0% (lower is better)	48.8%

	"A"-Rated Issues	"AA"-Rated Issues
The Morgan Bank		
Debt as a percent of net investment in plant (total outstanding long-term debt/net invested in plant [excl. cumulative depreciation])	90.0% (lower is better)	61.0%
Unrestricted current funds: net excess as a percent of fund expenses (excess of revenues over expenses [incl. R&E of auxiliary & athletics]/expenses)	2.0% (higher is better)	5.0%
Expendable fund balances as a percent of debt (all unrestricted & internally designated funds/outstanding long-term debt)	1.00 X (higher is better)	1.96 X
Unrestricted fund balance as a percent of debt (total current fund balance forward/outstanding long-term debt)	.80 X (higher is better)	1.08 X
Moody's (MHEFA)		
Debt service coverage—unrestricted current funds (excess of revenues over expenses [excl. debt service]/debt service)	1.5 X (higher is better)	2.0 X
Debt as a percent of plan (outstanding long-term debt/physical plant assets)	50.0% (lower is better)	20.0%

	"A"-Rated Issues	"AA"-Rated Issues
Debt as a percent of unrestricted endowment (outstanding long-term debt/quasi-endowment)	100.0% (lower is better)	50.0%
Debt as a percent of unrestricted endowment and operating fund balance (outstanding long-term debt/quasi-endowment plus total unrestricted current fund balance forward)	80.0% (lower is better)	40.0%

Appendix 5
Hospital and University Credit Ratings

Ratings awarded to hospital bond issues without credit substitution by Moody's Investors Service in 1985:

AA	10%
A1	28%
A	45%
BAA1	12%
BAA	5%
Under BAA	0%
	100%

Representative ratings awarded to hospital bond issues without credit substitution by Standard & Poor's Corporation in 1984:

AA	10%
A+	16%
A	34%
A−	30%
BBB+	10%
	100%

Source: Adams, Harkness & Hill, Inc.; Marsom B. Pratt, October 15, 1986.

College issues (648) without credit substitution currently rated by Standard & Poor's Corporation:

AAA	1%
AA+	4%
AA	14%
AA−	5%
A+	14%
A	38%
A−	10%
BBB+	7%
BBB	6%
BBB−	1%
	100%

Rating changes by Standard & Poor's Corporation:

Hospitals			
1984	11+	50−	
1985	11+	32−	
Colleges			
1984	2+	9−	
1985	8+	14−	
1986	7+	16−	(through September)

Appendix 6
Features of Tax-Exempt Financing Alternatives

Financing Alternatives	Maturity	Credit Support	Advantages/Disadvantages	
1. Tax-exempt commercial paper ("TXCP")	7–90 days	Revolving line of credit Letter of credit ("LOC")*	Advantages:	1. Maturities tailored to needs 2. Lowest interest rate 3. Lowest front end fees 4. Broadest investor market
			Disadvantages:	1. May not arbtirage proceeds 2. Continual reissuance; no stated long-term maturity
2. Daily demand bonds ("DDBs")	As desired/with daily "put"	LOC and standby	Advantages:	1. Maturities locked in 2. Tied to TXCP market 3. Proceeds can be arbitraged 4. Callable on 30 days notice 5. Wide market 6. Can be converted to fixed rate or packaged with an interest-rate swap

* Letter of credit: Commitment by a commercial bank to honor demands for payment of a debt.

Financing Alternatives	Maturity	Credit Support	Advantages/Disadvantages
			Disadvantages: 1. Bonds "put" must be remarketed—frequency of "put" 2. Unremarketed bonds placed with standby bank for a fee 3. Paying agent, registrar fees higher than for TXCP
3. Variable rate demand notes ("VRDN")	Discretionary/usually a 7-day "put"	LOC and standby	Advantages: 1. Long-term and interim maturities locked in 2. Attractive short-term rate 3. Callable on 30 days notice 4. Wide market 5. Can be converted to fixed rate or packaged with an interest-rate swap
			Disadvantages: 1. Bonds "put" must be remarketed 2. Unremarketed bonds placed with standby bank for a fee 3. Paying agent, registrar

				fees higher than for TXCP & ''DDBs''
4. Flexible variable rate demand notes (''Flex VRDNs'')	As desired/with daily, 7-day, 1 month, 3 month, 6 month, or annual ''put''	Daily through 3 months—LOC and standby 6-month or annual—none/assumes MIG-1**	Advantages:	1. Flexibility to change ''put'' period to take advantage of short-term interest-rate movements
5. Quarterly tender notes	As desired/with 3-month ''put''	Assumes MIG-1 or LOC and standby	Advantages:	1. Maturities locked in 2. 90-day rate 3. Insulation from short swings in interest 4. Can be converted to fixed rate or packaged with an interest-rate swap
			Disadvantages:	1. Callable only on 90 days notice 2. Bonds ''put'' must be remarketed 3. Unremarketed bonds placed with standby bank for a fee
6. Annual tender notes	As desired/with annual ''put''	None	Advantages:	1. Maturities locked in 2. 1-year rate 3. Insulation from short swings in interest

** MIG-1: Moody's Investment Grade 1.

Financing Alternatives	Maturity	Credit Support	Advantages/Disadvantages	
				4. Infrequency of "puts" 5. No letter of credit 6. Can be converted to fixed rate or packaged with an interest-rate swap
			Disadvantages:	1. Callable only once without a premium per year 2. Rates could be high during rate-setting period
7. Fixed-rate notes	6 months, 1 year	None	Advantages:	1. Fixed rate of interest over fiscal year 2. No letter of credit
			Disadvantages:	1. Higher cost of borrowing today 2. Usually noncallable 3. Investor market less broad
8. "Put" bonds	1, 2, 3, 5 years	None, assumes credit-worthy rating	Advantages:	1. Taps intermediate market for long-term maturities
			Disadvantages:	1. Interest-rate risk when remarketing
9. Long-term fixed-rate debt	10–30 years	None, credit of issuer or issuance	Advantages:	1. Known, certain rate of interest

				2. Can hedge or swap without "put" exposure 3. Can utilize sophisticated marketing
			Disadvantages:	1. Higher interest rates
10. Pooled capital financings	5–30 years	Required LOC or insurance and line of credit	Advantages:	1. Economies of scale 2. Credit homogenization
			Disadvantages:	1. Rebate requirement
11. Taxable commercial paper	Mostly 30–45 days (sold on a discounted basis)	Letter of credit probably required	Advantages:	1. Low interest rates, broad market
			Disadvantages:	1. Large program with active management generally required 2. Reissuance risk
12. Medium-term notes	9 months to 15 years	None	Advantages:	1. Flexible 2. Broad market 3. Generally noncallable. 4. Can average interest costs 5. Extend short-term borrowings when rates are volatile
			Disadvantages:	1. Higher rates than commercial paper 2. Sold on "best efforts" basis 3. Official statement required

Financing Alternatives	Maturity	Credit Support	Advantages/Disadvantages
13. U.S. domestic public market	1–30 years	None	Advantages: 1. Large issues possible 2. Call flexibility 3. Quick access to market Disadvantages: 1. Rate may be above foreign
14. Private placement	$5–50 million 5–25 years	None	Advantages: 1. Quick access to market 2. Small sizes easily issued 3. Delayed funding available Disadvantages: 1. Large deals (over $100MM) not always cost effective 2. Stricter call provisions 3. Larger maturities limited 4. Limited distribution
15. Foreign currency denominated bonds	Somewhat shorter than U.S. bonds	Same as U.S.	Advantages: 1. Lower total interest cost possible 2. May be attractive arbitrage advantages 3. Quick delivery Disadvantages: 1. Legal—possible for issuer? 2. Shorter maturities than U.S. 3. Currency risk 4. Need for name recognition

Appendix 7

Significant Features of the Tax Reform Act of 1986

Bonds of state and political subdivisions are generally considered either governmental use bonds or private activity bonds. Governmental use bonds are usually exempt from federal income tax, but private activity bonds are subject to tax unless they fit into one of a number of categories designated qualified private activity bonds. Qualified private activity bonds are subject to more severe limitations than governmental use bonds in establishing and maintaining their tax exemption, except for qualified 501(c)(3) bonds. Qualified 501(c)(3) bonds, although designated qualified private activity bonds, are, in many cases, exempted from the tests applicable to private activity bonds and treated more like governmental use bonds.

In the Tax Reform Act of 1986, tests to distinguish between governmental use bonds and private activity bonds have been changed. Rather than the 25 percent trade or business test and the 25 percent security interest test in the old law, there is now a 10 percent trade or business test and a 10 percent security interest test. Consequently, the new law permits considerably less private involvement in public projects financed with tax-exempt bonds.

Public higher education institutions' issues generally fall under the category of governmental use bonds, and private institutions' issues usually are qualified 501(c)(3) bonds. This produces tremendous inequality of treatment between public and private higher education institutions. Public institutions are allowed virtually unlimited access to the tax-exempt market (subject only to those restrictions applicable to governmental use bonds such as rebate of excess arbitrage profits). Private universities are subject to the provisions applicable to qualified 501(c)(3) bonds, which include most significantly a cap on tax-exempt financing of $150 million outstanding at any time.

Ed. note: Reprinted in part, with permission, from David C. Clapp, "Tax Reform and the Bond Market," in Richard E. Anderson and Joel Meyerson, eds., *Financing Higher Education: Strategies after Tax Reform* (San Francisco: Jossey-Bass, 1987).

According to a report issued by the Task Force on Higher Education Finance (1986), such a cap will cause more than twenty-five private universities to lose access to the tax-exempt market. At the same time, public institutions, regardless of volume, will be allowed the financial advantage. Such a restriction is an arbitrary, yet significant, discrimination among schools. With interest rate differentials of as much as 4 percent between taxable and nontaxable debt instruments, competitive advantage could result for public institutions. This is a double blow to private institutions, which already suffer from the weakening of charitable contributions. Many private institutions may have to forego much needed maintenance and rehabilitation for their significantly older campuses. The cap also ignores the fact that although educational institutional needs for capital are relatively small, they are vital to the educational system in the United States and should not be denied complete tax-exempt status.

The average volume of debt issued for 501(c)(3) organizations in 1983, 1984, and 1985 of $14.2 billion will be cut to approximately $6.3 billion, based on figures from reports of the Task Force on Higher Education Finance (1986).

Certain state or local governmental universities and hospitals (including certain public benefit corporations) also have been classified as tax exempt under Section 501(c)(3). To the extent that such an entity is a governmental unit or an agency or instrumentality of a governmental unit (as determined under present law), bonds for the entity would be treated as governmental bonds rather than as qualified 501(c)(3) bonds.

Furthermore, certain facilities eligible for financing with qualified 501(c)(3) bonds may comprise part of a larger facility otherwise ineligible for such financing, or portions of a section 501(c)(3) organization facility may be used for activities of persons other than section 501(c)(3) organizations or governmental units. The Treasury Department may adopt rules for allocating the costs of such mixed-use facilities (including common elements) according to any reasonable method that properly reflects the proportionate benefit to be derived by the various users of the facility. Only the portions of such mixed-use facilities owned and used by section 501(c)(3) organizations could be financed with tax-exempt bonds.

Five Percent Private Activity Limit and Costs of Issuance

Another provision of the new tax law that affects both private and public institutions of higher education is the 5 percent rule. This rule states that no more than 5 percent of the proceeds of an issue may be used for trade or business with a nongovernmental entity. Should the limit be exceeded, the bonds will be deemed taxable retroactive to the date of issue. In addition, all costs of issuance must be taken from that same 5 percent, and those costs may not exceed 2 percent. Thus, the percentage available for private activity will be even less than 5 percent. Additionally, the 2 percent cost of issuance may prove very difficult for issuers with smaller projects. This provision will obviously affect the way universities do business, particularly relating to food services, financial aid services, and research. Insurance premiums and letter of credit fees may, however, be deemed interest expense rather than cost of issuance.

This limitation on private use poses special problems for research universities that enter into cooperative research agreements with for-profit organizations. State and other governmental universities are similarly restricted, but at the higher 10 percent exclusion.

There is no restriction on using bond-financed property to perform general (as opposed to product-development) research supported or sponsored by a for-profit organization as part of a cooperative research arrangement. Similarly, any cooperative research agreement that provides that the sponsoring organization have access to the resulting technology on the same basis as any third party should not jeopardize tax-exempt status. Thus, a cooperative research agreement that provides a license of any resulting technology at a royalty rate fixed in advance of the performance of the research could constitute such a trade or business use. However, an agreement with only a first right of refusal (at a competitive price) for the sponsoring person would probably not constitute such a use. This raises the issue of whether business-sponsored research projects that are not purely for charity will be cost effective for the business.

Arbitrage Requirements and Reserve Restrictions

. . . arbitrage requirements, including rebate of arbitrage profits previously applicable only to industrial development bonds, will now apply to all tax-exempt bonds, including governmental use bonds. Thus, private and public higher education institutions will not be able to retain any investment earnings on bond proceeds in excess of the bond yield. (This provision excludes costs of issuance, which generally would make the bond yield and permissible investment rate higher.) Earnings must be calculated each year, and excess earnings must be rebated every five years. Furthermore, the minor portion of proceeds that may be invested at an unrestricted yield would be reduced from the present 15 percent (which includes a reasonably required reserve) to the lesser of 5 percent of bond proceeds or $100,000 (not including a reserve fund). A reserve fund is generally limited to 10 percent of proceeds unless the reserve is funded by nonbond issue proceeds, in which case those funds do not count against the 10 percent limit. The reserve fund is, nevertheless, subject to the same arbitrage requirements. Even for a temporary period of three years, arbitrage profits must be rebated; the temporary period rules only provide a respite for the administrative burdens of dealing with restricted yield investments.

Refundings

Interest rates rise and fall in line with market forces. If, after debt is issued, interest rates should fall significantly, the issuer may wish to refinance the old debt at a lower rate. New debt issued to retire old debt before it is due is called advanced refunding.

The new tax law defines and restricts the type and number of permissible advance refundings. In general, pre-1986 bonds may be refunded twice and post-1986 bonds may be refunded only once. Unless already previously refunded, there are a number of other structural restrictions, including rules for calling bonds, temporary periods, and issuance expense.

The average maturity of bonds cannot exceed 120 percent of the average reasonably expected economic life of the assets financed, and 501(c)(3) bonds will have to be approved by an elected public official after a public hearing. . . .

Miscellaneous Tax-Exempt Items

Alternative Minimum Tax. Neither governmental education bond issues nor qualified 501(c)(3) institutions should be subject to the corporate or individual alternative minimum tax (AMT). This is good news because debt that is subject to AMT must offer a higher interest rate to attract investors.

Cost of Carry. The new tax bill eliminates the 80 percent deduction for interest expenses incurred by financial institutions to purchase or carry tax-exempt bonds acquired after August 1986, although there is an exception for bonds issued by a small issuer that does not issue more than $10 million a year. This provision will raise the cost of issuance and dilute the market for tax-exempt debt.

Appendix 8
Example: Choosing a Source of Funds

Assume that the college has received a gift of $10 million. It could be:

1. invested in the endowment with a return of 6 percent to be paid out annually;
2. invested as above, but with the 6 percent used to service debt that has a net interest rate of 7½ percent—debt is used to construct the building costing $10 million.

Assume that operating and maintenance expenses are $250,000 per year, and 25 percent of building costs are to be used for new research projects so that a portion of interest and depreciation can be recovered each year.

Whether building with debt is more favorable than building with cash depends on the relationship between the interest rate on the debt and the return on the funds. Given a return of 6 percent, building with debt will always dominate building with cash if the interest rate on the debt is less than 3½ percent; when the interest rate is 7½ percent, building with debt will dominate building with cash if the return on the endowment is more than 8.9 percent. The tradeoff between not building and building with cash on the one hand, and not building and building with debt on the other, depends on the value of having the facility versus its immediate effect on the budget. The value could be defensive, because not replacing the asset could mean lost revenue.

Ed. note: Example courtesy of Lyn Hutton of the University of Southern California and Bill Massy of Stanford University.

To summarize the example:

Decision	Known Outcomes		
	Building available	Budget impact	Ending capital
A. Don't build	No	+$0.6 million	$10 million
B. Build with debt	Yes	−$0.5 million*	$10 million
C. Build with cash	Yes	−$0.25 million	$0

* Investment income of $0.6 million plus cost recoveries of $0.25 million less $1.1 million annual debt service (includes principal and interest at 10 percent amortized over 25 years), less $250,000 of operating and maintenance expense.

Appendix 9
Example: Capitalization of Interest

The following example illustrates the application of these concepts in the situation described below:

A. The entity is committed to construct Project A at a cost of $10 million. Project A is to be financed from three sources:
   1. a $4 million government grant restricted to use for the specified construction project, payable $1 million per year;
   2. a $4 million tax-exempt borrowing at an interest rate of 8 percent ($320,000 per year); and
   3. $2 million from operations.

B. The entity has $10 million in other borrowings that are outstanding throughout the construction of Project A. The interest rate on those borrowings is 6 percent. Other qualifying assets of the entity never exceed $5 million during the construction of Project A.

C. The proceeds from the borrowing and the initial phase of the grant are received one year in advance of starting construction of Project A and are temporarily invested in interest-bearing investments yielding 12 percent. Interest income earned from temporary investments is not reinvested.

D. Project A will take four years after start of construction to complete.

E. The table below sets forth the amount of interest to be capitalized as part of the entity's investment in Project A.

F. Over the course of construction the net cost of financing is $678,000, the sum of the interest capitalized for the five years. Accordingly, the entity's total net investment in Project A will be $10,678,000.

	19X1	19X2	19X3	19X4	19X5
	(amounts in thousands)				
(1) Assumed average qualifying assets	$ 0	$2,000	$5,000	$8,000	$9,000
(2) Average funding received					
borrowing	4,000	4,000	4,000	4,000	4,000
grant	1,000	2,000	3,000	4,000	4,000

	19X1	19X2	19X3	19X4	19X5
		(amounts in thousands)			
(3) Average temporary investments ((2) − (1), not less than zero)*					
borrowing	4,000	3,000	1,000	0	0
grant	1,000	1,000	1,000	0	0
(4) Interest earned ((3) × 12 percent)					
(a) borrowing	480	360	120	0	0
(b) grant	120	120	120	0	0
(5) Average qualifying assets in excess of borrowing, grant, and interest earned on grant**	0	0	0	0	640
(6) Interest cost capitalized— other borrowings ((5) × 6 percent)	0	0	0	0	38
(7) Interest cost—tax exempt borrowings	320	320	320	320	320
(8) Interest capitalized ((6) + (7) − (4)(a))***	(160)	(40)	200	320	358

* Balances of unexpended borrowings and unexpended grants can vary depending on the source from which the entity elects to disburse funds.
** That is, (1) average qualifying assets minus the sum of [(2) average funding received plus (4)(b) cumulative interest earned on grant], not less than zero.
*** Note that amounts in parentheses are reductions in the cost of the asset.
Source: Statement of Financial Accounting Standards (SFAS) no. 62.

Appendix 10
Example: Gain on "Low to High" Refunding

Statement of Financial Accounting Standards (SFAS) no. 76 defines the circumstances in which debt may be considered extinguished for financial reporting purposes. Accounting Principles Board (APB) Opinion no. 26 requires immediate recognition of a gain or loss when there is an extinguishment. AICPA Statement of Position (SOP) 78-5 (now superseded by SFAS no. 76) discusses the calculation of the gain or loss.

In general, a gain or loss arises from (1) the write-off of unamortized issuance costs and debt discount, (2) any premium that is required to call the old debt, and (3) in an advance refunding, the difference between the interest rate that must be paid on the old debt and the interest earned on the escrow fund itself (which generally must be equal to the rate on the new debt, under IRS regulations).

For example, assume the XYZ College wishes to refund $40 million of sinking-fund facilities debt. Although current interest rates, at 10 percent, are higher than the 7 percent coupon on the old debt, extended maturities are available that significantly reduce XYZ's immediate cash outflow for debt service. Four years remain before the first date on which the old debt may be called, at a 1 percent premium. The old debt was issued at ½ percent discount. The gain would be calculated as follows:

New Debt		
Principal	$38,000,000	
Issuance Costs	(1,100,000)	
		$36,900,000
Old Debt		
Principal	$40,000,000	
Unamortized issuance costs	(900,000)	
Unamortized discount	(360,000)	
Call premium	(400,000)	
		38,340,000
Gain on refunding		$ 1,440,000

Entries on the books for this transaction would be as follows:

A. Booking of original debt at the time of its issuance (simplified):

Academic plant	$38,600,000	
Issue costs	1,000,000	
Discount	400,000	
Old debt		$40,000,000

B. Record refunding, including gain, in the plant fund:

Old debt	$40,000,000	
Issue costs—new debt	1,100,000	
New debt		$38,000,000
Issue costs—old debt		900,000
Discount—old debt		360,000
Reserve for call premium		400,000
Fund balance		1,440,000

C. Each year the mandatory transfer from the current fund would be the amount necessary to service the new debt:

Mandatory transfer for debt service	$4,500,000	
Cash		$4,500,000

D. Eventually equity would build up in the plant fund equal to the value of the academic plant:

Buildings	$38,600,000	
Gain		$ 1,440,000
Retirement of principal		38,000,000
Amortization of issuance costs		(1,100,000)
Amortization of issuance costs and discount—old issue		(140,000)
Call premium		400,000

Notes

Preface

1. This amount is greater than the aggregate growth in university endowments during the period, as measured in the respective NACUBO endowment studies. It suggests that American higher education may soon be a net debtor, meaning that at some time investors may hold more college and university issues than the securities owned by college endowments.

2. Harvey H. Kaiser, "Capital Needs in Higher Education," *Financing Higher Education: Strategies after Tax Reform*, ed. Richard E. Anderson and Joel W. Meyerson (San Francisco: Jossey-Bass, 1987). Other studies have suggested that $10 billion may be needed to renew university research assets alone.

3. A bibliography of debt-related articles appears in appendix 3.

Chapter 1 History of College Debt

1. The material on the history of college debt is described in more detail in Patricia A. Leary, "Historical Perspective on University Debt Financing," *Creative Financing for Higher Education Facilities and Equipment* (Denver, Colo.: State Higher Education Executive Officers Association, 1985), pp. 1-16.

2. Donaldson, Lufkin & Jenrette, "Financing Higher Education: Life after Tax Reform," presentation at NACUBO Annual Meeting, July 1987.

Chapter 2 The Need for New Debt

1. Jane Perlez, "New York School Buildings Scarred by Years of Neglect," *New York Times*, May 13, 1987.

Chapter 3 Common Concerns with Debt

1. For a more thorough discussion of integrated financial planning, see William F. Massy, "Making It All Work: Sound Financial Management," in *Financing Higher Education after Tax Reform*, ed. Richard E. Anderson and Joel Meyerson (San Francisco: Jossey-Bass, 1987).

2. See Robert Heilbroner, "The Deficit," *New Yorker*, July 30, 1984, pp. 47-55.

3. The difference between financial and physical capital is explained in a 1986 NACUBO monograph on capital maintenance by Daniel D. Robinson. See *Capital Maintenance for Colleges and Universities* (Washington, D.C.: NACUBO, 1986).

4. Regina E. Herzlinger and William S. Krasker, "Who Profits from Non-Profits?" *Harvard Business Review*, January/February 1987.

5. A. M. Woodruff, "1980-95: The Threat to Higher Education: Special Reference to Connecticut," Ford Foundation, New York, May 1979.

Chapter 4 Choosing a Source of Funds

1. Of course, investments may earn 12 percent, while the board chooses to distribute only 6 percent. For the good of the overall institution, the earnings rate should enter this choice. This is one reason debt is centrally managed.

2. Rating agencies are discouraging the accumulation of variable-rate debt on college balance sheets.

3. The relevant ratios will change, of course, as depreciation finds its way into college financial statements. One critical new measure will then be the age of the plant—the "reserve ratio" of accumulated depreciation to gross assets.

4. Donaldson, Lufkin & Jenrette, "Financing Higher Education: Life after Tax Reform," presentation at NACUBO Annual Meeting, July 1987.

Chapter 5 Credit Support

1. David C. Clapp, "What's New in Debt Financing in Higher Education," presentation at the Symposium on New Ideas on Capital Financing, sponsored by the Forum for College Financing Alternatives, October 20, 1986.

Chapter 6 The Effect of the Tax Reform Act

1. Donaldson, Lufkin & Jenrette, "Financing Higher Education: Life after Tax Reform," presentation at NACUBO Annual Meeting, July 1987.

2. Ibid.

3. David C. Clapp, "What's New in Debt Financing in Higher Education," presentation at the Symposium on New Ideas on Capital Financing, sponsored by the Forum for College Financing Alternatives, October 20, 1986.

4. Donaldson, Lufkin & Jenrette, "Financing Higher Education."

5. Clapp, "What's New in Debt Financing."

6. David C. Clapp, "Tax Reform and the Bond Market," in *Financing Higher Education after Tax Reform*, ed. Richard E. Anderson and Joel Meyerson (San Francisco: Jossey-Bass, 1987), p. 40.